MAKING A WAY

ULYSSES BYAS,

First Black School Superintendent
in the Southeast, and His Fight
for Educational Reform

by

Marilyn Robinson

InspiringVoices®
A Service of **Guideposts**

Inspiring Voices books may be ordered through booksellers or by contacting:

Inspiring Voices
1663 Liberty Drive
Bloomington, IN 47403
www.inspiringvoices.com
1 (866) 697-5313

ISBN: 978-1-4624-0791-0 (sc)
ISBN: 978-1-4624-0790-3 (e)

Library of Congress Control Number: 2013920840

Printed in the United States of America.

Inspiring Voices rev. date: 12/16/2013

To my husband, Paul Robinson Jr.

And to Ulysses Byas's wife, Annamozel Byas.

Contents

List of Illustrations

Preface

Dr. Byas has been my mentor and friend since 1968. Our paths first crossed when I took a job with the Georgia Teachers and Education Association (GTEA). At that time, two teachers associations still existed in Georgia: the Georgia Education Association and the GTEA, which was started by black educators at a time when they were excluded from the Georgia Education Association (GEA). I was a white teacher looking for work in Atlanta after two years of classroom teaching, when I met Dr. Horace Tate, the executive director of the GTEA. After conversing awhile, he offered me the position of director of research and publications at GTEA. I was young, white, naïve, and idealistic. Green as grass. Ulysses Byas was also a new employee at GTEA, and he was a black, middle-aged, experienced school administrator who was "seasoned" in the ways of segregation politics. He became my colleague, mentor, and friend.

Over the next two years, we worked together on various projects, including the coauthoring of magazine articles about educational issues facing black teachers and the association. In 1970, the GTEA and GEA merged, becoming the Georgia Association of Educators. Mr. Byas left shortly after the merger to accept the position of superintendent of schools in Macon County, Alabama—Tuskegee is the county seat—and I left to work with the nascent Atlanta Street Academy as a teacher and college prep advisor. Three years later, with the status of the Street Academy in jeopardy, I went to Macon County, Alabama, and applied for work with my former mentor. There I worked with three federal projects, assisted with Mr. Byas's research for his doctoral dissertation, and resumed our friendship. In 1977, we again went in different directions, with him moving to a superintendency in Long Island, New York, and me getting married and becoming a teacher in Columbus, Georgia.

Years later, when Dr. Byas retired, he and his wife moved back to his first hometown, Macon, Georgia, and we embarked on this project soon after. Beginning in 2002, Dr. Byas and I recorded several interviews in which he reviewed his years in Tuskegee, how he arrived there, what he found, what happened, and why he ultimately left. Having been there for the last three years of his tenure, I was aware of some of this story but had never known all of the details. In fact, the real reasons behind his decision to leave Tuskegee were not known to anyone until many years later. The story is rather dramatic and is detailed in chapter 5.

Dr. Byas's tenure at Macon County Schools, 1970–1976, was critical to the health of that school system. The issues he tackled were manifold and tricky. Some he attacked directly, but many required other tactics. The white students had exited the system to attend the new "segregation academy" supported and encouraged by the George C. Wallace government. Many of these students had family members still working with the public schools. Supplies and materials purchased with public funds were disappearing, and it was strongly suspected that they were being siphoned to the private school. Rather than attack this problem "head on," Byas started instituting badly needed systems of accountability: systems that were fiscally wise as well as politically wise. By this flanking tactic, the problem of disappearing supplies was drastically curtailed. In the light of current practice, Byas's policies and innovations may seem obvious, but at that time and in that place, these policies instituted large and small changes, which many people supported and applauded. No doubt, others felt the sting of losing their hold on practices and powers that they had enjoyed for years.

Another tactic that Byas used to the advantage of the school system was his penchant for networking. Byas gained many admirers inside and outside the educational establishment. Some of these people were vital links to the US Department of Education and assisted in getting grants for Macon County. As he describes it, the first few years in Tuskegee were also years of strong support from the Alabama Department of Education. Nevertheless, the Macon County School System was under scrutiny. Even the superintendent's salary was limited by state restrictions. When the issue of the Alabama Educational Television Network came up, things took a decided turn. This story is still only dimly understood, but the shadowy influence of opposition and oppression became more visible. With auditors in perpetual attendance and with women picketing the administration offices day after day, the employees were aware that something strange was happening. However, we did not know why this was so. Not until Dr. Byas told his story to a group of supporters in the 1990s did anyone know the context of this opposition and his decision to leave Macon County without a fight.

Dr. Byas brought all the necessary skills and attitudes to his role as superintendent. How many others would have known how to examine a school as a carpenter would? How many would have crawled under the building as he did at the Prairie Farms School to observe the termite damage? How many people had the ability to also create accountability systems and to work with his opponents without either bullying or caving in? How many could come up with a strategy to test the honesty and loyalty of employees without confrontation? How many would have had the spiritual guidance and strength to speak out in spite of knowing his job could be jeopardized? How many could hold their own counsel for more than twenty years? Who would be so concerned about the welfare of a couple who had deceived him thirty years ago that he would withhold their names to this day? How many black people could accept and work with white people, knowing that many white people were racists and unwilling to change?

Dr. Byas possessed all these abilities and more. That is why I admire him as one of the greatest mentors in my life.

NOTE: Dr. Byas died in 2012.

Acknowledgments

There comes a point at which you look around and realize that a long project is about to come to fruition. This point in the process of writing this book has finally dawned for me. Wow! This book is actually going to be completed! So now it is time to look backward to all the people who have made it possible to achieve this goal. How can I remember everyone? How can I put into words the meaning of their support? Each author works diligently to thank his or her helpers. So I too have come to this point. I confess to being somewhat overwhelmed at the enormity of the task.

First and foremost, this book was the conception of Dr. Byas, and it represents a large piece of his life. I have tried to faithfully record his words and ideas as expressed in numerous interviews as well as our years of friendship. It is my hope that those who know him will recognize his spirit here. Thank you for entrusting your story to me.

Secondly, my husband, Paul, and Dr. Byas's wife, Annamozel, have been loyal supporters and made our lengthy interviews possible with their quiet presence. In addition to several trips to Macon, Paul accompanied me to Tuskegee and Montgomery, where I interviewed three former school board members.

Thanks, of course, to those board members—Dr. Ellis Hall, Dr. J. H. M. Henderson, and Mrs. Consuello Harper—for their willingness to share their time and their memories with me.

My sister, Jean Pajot Forrester, designed the cover for this book and gave many words of encouragement along the way.

Dr. Richard Davies not only shared many hints about publishing this book, he generously took on the task of formatting it when I was simply overwhelmed by the computer skills I needed but did not possess. I am not overstating it when I say that this book might not have been completed without his support.

Over the years of development, several friends have read all or parts of the manuscript, and many have listened patiently as I fumed about my seeming inability to move beyond the point of research to getting a readable story on paper. Although they will remain nameless, lest I omit someone who deserves my thanks, I appreciate each one for the invaluable but intangible support they gave me.

Despite this support over the years, I alone am responsible for any errors that may have crept into this manuscript. I hope that very few escaped our scrutiny, but as it is a human enterprise, I imagine there will be some. For these, I ask the readers' forgiveness.

INTRODUCTION
Tuskegee before 1970

Tuskegee, Alabama, the county seat of Macon County, holds a special place in the culture and history of black people and in the civil rights movement in Alabama and throughout the United States. It was not surprising that it hired the first black superintendent of a county school system in the United States.

Tuskegee is the county seat of Macon County, which is essentially a rural area. In the 1970s, its population was about 25,000 people. It is situated in the east-central section of Alabama, approximately forty miles east of Montgomery, Alabama, and forty miles west of Columbus, Georgia. It is large in area: 616 square miles. It has several small communities located around the central city of Tuskegee: Shorter to the west, Notasulga to the north, and smaller areas served by their own schools to the east (Nichols) and south (South Macon).[1]

Shortly after the end of the Civil War, white Macon Countians began to reassert their power over the county, despite the activities of the Radical Republicans in Washington and the local black leadership. For example, the home of a black Republican leader, James Alston, was attacked with gunfire in 1870, injuring both Alston and his wife. The incident led to armed conflict between the black and white communities.[2] A constant tension ensued here and all across the South as blacks sought to migrate away from the area while white property owners sought to keep the blacks available as a source of labor while also regaining white political and economic control of the region.[3]

In Macon County and all across the South, whites did regain control through violence, intimidation, and economic serfdom through the "crop lien system" or sharecropping. When federal troops were finally withdrawn from the former rebel states in a deal that gave Rutherford B. Hayes the presidency, the fate of the recently freed slaves hardened into nearly permanent vassalage.[4]

The fate of Tuskegee and Macon County might have slipped into the swamp of anonymity that swallowed most of the South, had it not been for the creation of a "colored high school" in 1881 under the initial leadership of Lewis Adams, a local tinsmith. But this school, established with the support of white politicians and merchants, Arthur Brooks and Wilbur Foster, later became the renowned Tuskegee Institute under the leadership of Booker T. Washington and George Washington Carver.[5] With this partnership established by the school and community, Tuskegee entered an era of calmer race relationships. However, the seeds for future discord were also sown with the growth of the educated, middle-class black community in Tuskegee. Washington was convinced that political power would follow from economic power, which he was determined to develop through education.

Despite the growth of Tuskegee Institute and the national influence of Dr. Washington, white political control of Alabama and Macon County grew stronger. Although the Macon County population was overwhelmingly black, only sixty-five blacks were registered voters in the early 1900s, thanks to the new state constitution, which disenfranchised many thousands of black and white citizens by forcing them to prove their literacy, employment, or ownership of property valued at $300. A poll tax was also enacted, and the local board of registrars was created with wide discretion to enforce these requirements.[6]

While the white citizens of Macon County insisted that they lived in a model community, black citizens were deprived of political power and much more. In fact, the funding for Tuskegee Institute, much of which came from Northern philanthropy, could hardly compensate for the immense difference in educational support from the local community, where white per pupil expenses were $65.18 in 1934, compared to only $6.58 for each black pupil.[7]

In 1923, at the urging of Tuskegee Institute President Robert R. Moton and white landowners anxious to sell their land, the US government built a Veterans Administration hospital for black soldiers from World War I. The hospital perpetuated a system of segregated care but benefited the Tuskegee community by the addition of many more black professionals. The staffing of the hospital by blacks was not without a fight. Whites saw the danger in having blacks in positions of authority as well as the loss of good-paying jobs, but Alabama law forbade whites to nurse blacks. The VA hospital ultimately provided 1,500 good-paying federal jobs for blacks, jobs over which white Macon Countians had no control.[8]

Thus, by 1940, more than one thousand black, middle-class professionals lived and worked in Tuskegee, where they formed the "model neighborhood" of Greenwood and sent their children to the "model public school" known as Children's House on the Tuskegee Institute campus.[9]

Not surprisingly, the leadership for change in Macon County first emerged from the faculty at Tuskegee Institute. Charles Gomillion, a young teacher, was insulted when a merchant called him "Preacher," after which he vowed not to do his shopping in local stores. At age twenty-eight, Gomillion discovered that in 1928 there were only thirty-two black registered voters in the area, all of whom were administrators at the Tuskegee Institute or the VA Hospital or owned businesses. In other words, none of these voters owed their jobs and economic welfare to the white community.[10] Gomillion became the leader of the Tuskegee Civic Association (TCA) that led a long-running battle with the board of registrars and the state of Alabama over the right of blacks to register and vote, culminating in the 1960s. Throughout this struggle, white conservatives clung to power by means fair and foul.

In January 1941, another significant national event made a tremendous impact on the community. At the urging of Tuskegee Institute President Frederick Patterson, the community was selected as the training site for black airmen. The introduction of black airmen from all parts of the nation, many having never encountered the form of racism known as segregation, created much tension and eventual violence. The trigger was the question of who was responsible for policing these outsiders when they left the military base and went into the town. A confrontation in April 1942 over custody of a drunken soldier led to fighting and a near riot before a compromise was struck.[11]

Throughout the New Deal and World War II, white conservatives felt threatened by the policies of Franklin Roosevelt and by Supreme Court decisions of the following decades. In Tuskegee, the TCA began a campaign to unseat Sheriff Pat Evans, whose regime of brutality resulted in the death of Walter Gunn in 1942.[12] Although the white primary was also struck down in the 1940s by the US Supreme Court (*Smith v. Allwright*), the actions of the Macon County Board of Registrars continued to prevent blacks from registering. For example, in July 1945, while 200 blacks waited in line to register, ninety of their applications were taken but only ten were approved.[13] When court cases ensued, registrars either resigned to avoid being arrested or went into hiding so that potential black voters would not know where to go to register, even using nongovernmental locations like the general store owned by a known antiblack leader.

In 1948, Governor Folsom, a reputed liberal, appointed a registrar who actually accepted black registrations. W. H. Bentley from Notasulga was responsible for increasing black registration from about 100 to over 400 in one year, whereupon the other two registrars stopped attending meetings, effectively halting further registrations.[14] Nevertheless, by 1950, black voters made up 30 percent of the electorate as compared to 73 percent of the population of the county[15] and succeeded in defeating Sheriff Evans.

The gulf between white expectations and black desires continued to grow, and attitudes of people on the extremes hardened, while more liberal or realistic whites and blacks worked toward compromise. One example of the hardening of attitudes and practices was the effort by local politician Sam Engelhardt, newly elected to the Alabama legislature from the Shorter community in western Macon County. He wrote a bill to close all public schools if the US Supreme Court outlawed segregation of schools. Although the bill failed by a 2:1 margin, it was indicative of the thinking of some people.[16]

In January of 1951, the issue of school desegregation changed from "if" to "now" when a black parent asked the school board to provide a course in geometry for her son at Tuskegee Institute High School, the school for blacks, or to allow him to enroll at Tuskegee High School, the white school. When the request was denied, the TCA began to circulate a petition on behalf of the family, but the issue went unresolved. Then in 1954, a black woman named Jessie Parkhurst Guzman, a Tuskegee Institute professor, ran for a position on the school board, losing 3:1 in a vote that mirrored the racial makeup of the electorate.[17]

Problems relating to voter registration continued, as the county moved in fits and starts toward opening up the process. When the Alabama legislature removed the cumulative feature of the poll tax in 1953, for example, the cost of registering was reduced to that of the current year only. The new governor, "Big Jim" Folsom, an avowed liberal, threatened Sam Engelhardt, saying he would "register every damn nigger in the county." Although his efforts fell far short, progress was made in that direction.[18]

Following the announcement of the US Supreme Court *Brown* decision in 1954, a group of thirty-two blacks informed the board of education that they would submit a desegregation petition as part of the National Association for the Advancement of Colored People's (NAACP) national plan. When Engelhardt introduced a bill allowing the board of education to fire any teacher who advocated desegregation, the bill was passed by the legislature but vetoed by Gov. Folsom. Folsom also reappointed Herman Bentley to the board of registrars, but Bentley died in 1955 and the board was not reconstituted until 1957.[19]

During the Montgomery bus boycott of the same period, however, Folsom sat on his hands. Whatever liberal leanings the governor had had, he lost his nerve or changed his mind as the civil rights movement heated up.

Meanwhile, Engelhardt seemed to be gaining strength in his opposition to desegregation. In 1957, the senator introduced a bill to redraw Tuskegee's city limits in such a way as to exclude all but twelve black voters. Charles Gomillion and the TCA held a meeting attended by 3,000 people (500 were able to get inside and the remainder stood outside the church) where Engelhardt's bill was discussed. The outcome of the meeting was a "selective buying" campaign. Said Gomillion, "We are going to buy goods and services from those who help us, from those who make no effort to hinder us, from those who recognize us as first class citizens."[20] This campaign had an immediate impact on the merchants in Tuskegee, putting a fish market and the movie house out of business within a few days. By the spring of 1958, half of Tuskegee's white-owned retail businesses had failed. Some white merchants were reportedly ready to change their policies but feared the retaliation of Engelhardt and his supporters more than they feared economic losses.[21]

Senator Engelhardt was undeterred. In fact, he countered with a proposal to abolish Macon County completely by having it divided up and the territory annexed by surrounding counties. The fact that the surrounding counties didn't want large communities of black people and potential voters in their counties prevented the bill's passage.

Meanwhile, Alabama Attorney General John Patterson attempted to halt the boycott as unlawful. He attempted to intimidate local blacks by demanding membership rolls from the TCA, by questioning residents, and by making radio announcements. He had already chased organized NAACP activities from the state by imposing a fine of $100,000 on the organization when they would not submit membership lists. Although Patterson's actions failed to deter the TCA, he gained the spotlight in Tuskegee and won the governorship in 1958.[22]

The Tuskegee Civic Association was not intimidated by the machinations of Engelhardt and Patterson but might have actually been strengthened by them. Protests and meetings continued throughout the summer of 1957, drawing such noteworthy speakers as Martin Luther King Jr., Ralph David Abernathy, and Fred Shuttlesworth to the town. Indeed, the protests drew the attention of the national media, with stories carried by *Life, Time, Newsweek,* and *U.S. News & World Report.*[23]

Macon County and Tuskegee were controlled by five men from four prominent families, and they wanted to retain this control. An independent survey of white residents turned up many who said they feared black domination and blamed outside agitators and Russian Communists for the boycott. However, a significant minority believed that blacks deserved to have political rights.[24]

In February 1957, Charles Gomillion appeared before the US Senate Judiciary Committee and described the way whites were restricting black voters. The Civil Rights Act of 1957 had established the Civil Rights Division of the Department of Justice and the US Commission on Civil Rights. The latter agency began an investigation of the Tuskegee situation based on the data collected by the TCA. In the investigation, white public officials either denied knowledge of the circumstances or refused to answer altogether. The local registrars, ducking an order from federal district judge Frank M. Johnson to turn over voting records and to testify, simply resigned their positions. George C. Wallace, then a registrar in neighboring Barbour and Bullock counties, impounded his records to avoid bringing them to the commission hearings. Wallace made plenty of political hay out of this drama, infuriating Judge Johnson and gaining the name recognition and fame that would catapult him into the governorship. The commission's findings led to court cases against the local registrars, but their resignation again thwarted the process and no new registrars were appointed until July 1959. Those registrars promptly resigned and the fiasco was repeated the following year, prompting the TCA to request federal registrars.[25]

The Civil Rights Act of 1960 did not create federal registrars as the TCA had requested, but it did create federal referees appointed by federal judges. It also gave the Justice Department authority to sue states for denial of voting rights, leading to the reopening of the Macon County case under Judge Johnson. Although Governor Patterson appointed new registrars in Macon County, they continued to obstruct black applicants in the usual manner.

In 1960, the US Supreme Court ruled unanimously in *Gomillion v. Lightfoot* against the proposed gerrymandering of Macon County because the effect of the law was discriminatory. Then in March 1961, the Justice Department investigation ended with the finding that Macon County registrars had "deliberately engaged in acts and practices designed to discriminate against qualified Negroes." Johnson ordered the immediate registration of sixty-four blacks who had testified at the hearings, ordered the registrars to meet at least two days per month in the city of Tuskegee from 9:00 a.m. until 5:00 p.m. to examine at least six applicants at a time, to notify the applicants within twenty days of the results of their application with written reasons for any failure to qualify, and to present a detailed monthly report to him.[26]

As a result of these pressures for the registration of black voters, the election for local government in 1960 brought big changes, with new leadership that was not allied with Engelhardt. The buying boycott was gradually lifted, and meetings began occurring between the TCA and white liberals over the next few years. The ownership of the *Tuskegee News* changed hands from the ultraconservative Harold Fisher to Neil O. Davis, who had the backing of banker J. Allan Parker, a member of the biracial committee. The new city government built a swimming pool for blacks and the first public housing was constructed under their aegis.[27]

Throughout the early sixties, things seemed to be moving forward in terms of blacks and whites working together, attacking problems, and winning elections. By the summer of 1963, black voters numbered 3,000, approximately equal with white voters. An additional 6,000 blacks remained unregistered. But in 1962, the TCA decided to pay the legal expenses for a school desegregation court case, *Lee v. Macon County,* which was filed the following January by attorney Fred Gray. As a result of this desegregation suit, Judge Johnson ordered Macon County to desegregate Tuskegee High School when the new school year opened in September 1963 and to present a desegregation plan for the rest of the county by December. The city council, school board, and leading white liberals had decided not to oppose the order. The superintendent was C. A. Pruitt, who personally opposed the plan but went along with the order. Applications from black students who wanted to transfer to Tuskegee High School were accepted, and thirteen students were selected.[28]

Everything seemed to be in order until a meeting of the PTA held on the evening before school was to open. Conservatives hijacked the meeting, asking for Governor Wallace to be called in and the school opening to be postponed. One parent reported that Wallace had "offered to provide transportation for white students to other schools or to call a special session of the legislature to have Macon County's public schools closed." Another attendee, a state official whose home was in Montgomery, not Tuskegee, announced that "Montgomery" had a plan to close the public schools and organize a private school system.[29]

In fact, Governor Wallace did order the postponement of school for one week. The order was delivered to Tuskegee by a state trooper, and at 6:30 a.m. on the day school was scheduled to open, Tuskegee High School was ringed by 200 state troopers. Two white families attempted to walk through the lines with their children, only to be rebuffed. The following day, Sheriff Jim Clark from Selma, a town more than two hours away by car, and his posse mounted on horses appeared on the school grounds. The following Monday, when school was allowed to open, state troopers boarded the bus that was carrying the thirteen black students to Tuskegee High School and handed out an order from Gov. Wallace denying their entry into the school.[30]

The US Justice Department responded by taking out a restraining order to stop Wallace's interference. Wallace in turn called out the National Guard, whereupon President John F. Kennedy ordered the federalization of the Alabama National Guard and sent them back to their barracks. The following day, Tuskegee High School was desegregated along with schools in Birmingham.

Local opposition did not disappear, however. A group led by Frances Wadsworth asked Gov. Wallace to invoke a 1957 law that would allow school boards to close public schools and use the funds to operate private schools. Wallace agreed to support this movement. Meanwhile, of the 565 white students expected at the high school, only 125 arrived for classes when the school finally opened. Later that week, the football team voted to disband, and the following day, no white students remained at the high school. The grammar school located on the same property remained all white. Of the 565 white high school students, 130 transferred to Shorter High School and thirty-four transferred to Notasulga High School, both of which were then all white. Some students went to schools in neighboring counties or went to live with relatives in other cities, but most simply waited for the opening of the private school.[31]

Macon Academy was first opened in an abandoned mansion across the street from the public school. Donations for the school included $2,000 solicited by Gov. Wallace from state employees. By the time Ulysses Byas arrived in 1970, a building had been constructed on the edge of Tuskegee. By this time, the whites who had originally supported the desegregation effort had abandoned their efforts. Many of these more liberal whites suffered harassment and ostracism from their neighbors, including such acts as cross burnings, threatening phone calls, flattening of tires, and name-calling. The local white churches split because two of the liberal leaders were ministers. Social groups and even families were affected by these divisions. Some families moved out of the area completely.

The thirteen black students at Tuskegee High School worked hard and won the respect of their teachers (still all white), but they too were subjected to abusive phone calls and other forms of intimidation. Governor Wallace intervened again. The school board had been transporting the white students to Shorter and Notasulga High Schools until Judge Johnson ordered them to stop. So Wallace had the state board of education close Tuskegee High School by stating that its low student population was "not sufficient to justify paying the teachers." These thirteen black students were then transferred to Tuskegee Institute High School and the Macon County School Board was ordered by the state board to supply transportation for the white students attending Shorter and Notasulga High Schools.[32]

The TCA filed a complaint and requested that the federal courts order desegregation of all Alabama schools. Judge Johnson then ordered that the thirteen black students from Tuskegee High School be transferred to Shorter and Notasulga high schools. The situation at Shorter High School was calm, but trouble erupted when the black students arrived at Notasulga High School. A crowd had gathered, cursing the students on the bus. Selma's Sheriff Jim Clark and his mounted posse made another appearance. Clark assaulted a black photographer who had slipped onto the bus. The students were denied entry into the school. Judge Johnson again had to step in, forcing the entry of the black students. White students then withdrew from Notasulga High School and from Shorter. Most transferred to

Macon Academy. In April 1964, the school in Notasulga was defaced, and the following night, it was burned down.[33]

By the time of primary elections in August 1964, black voters outnumbered whites in Macon County. The TCA organized by precincts, hired poll workers, held candidate forums, and endorsed candidates in seven local races: four blacks and three whites, including Charles Gomillion who ran for a position on the board of education. All seven candidates won in the Democratic primary, which at that time was tantamount to winning the election, since there was no real Republican opposition.[34]

In the city of Tuskegee, white registered voters still held a slight majority (1,000 to 900). The TCA also endorsed candidates (four whites and two blacks) for city offices. Meanwhile, an organization called the Non-Partisan Voters League of Macon County (NPVL) developed a platform and a slate of candidates challenging TCA's gradualist and biracial approach. The NPVL won about 20 percent of the vote, forcing a runoff election. Nevertheless, TCA's two black candidates for city council won with white support. The new city government appointed blacks to municipal boards and committees, creating a truly interracial government for the first time in Tuskegee. It also created a community action committee, to seek and administer federal grants, and a biracial advisory committee.[35]

The school board was now chaired by Frances Rush, a liberal white woman who was known for her support of public education. Mr. Pruitt had resigned from the superintendency rather than face more problems with the desegregation efforts, and he was replaced with Joe Wilson. When the 1964–1965 school year started, Tuskegee High School had fifty-nine whites and fourteen blacks. By the end of the school year, the white enrollment had grown to 133. Meanwhile the private Macon Academy continued to grow and add new programs.[36]

But perhaps as significant, the split within the black community became more pronounced and open. The leader of the NPVL, Detroit Lee, ran for probate judge against the TCA candidate, Preston Hornsby, a white former sheriff who had replaced the brutal Sheriff Pat Evans with TCA support. During this period, young blacks around the nation were pushing for faster change. The Student Non-violent

Coordinating Committee (SNCC) organized a local chapter led by George Ware. Another student group, the Tuskegee Institute Advancement League, was formed to support the Selma movement. These students eventually began to protest the policies of the college and to organize protests against local merchants who did not hire blacks. They desegregated the "white" city pool on May 31, 1965, and the government closed it two days later. They also attempted to integrate the white Methodist Church but were denied entry. Within two weeks, 500 students demonstrated outside the church when they were again denied entry, leading to violence and arrests. They also worked in the rural areas to register local black voters.[37]

In July 1965 with the passage of the Voting Rights Act, Alabama had to stop giving literacy tests to prospective voters. The number of black voters continued to rise as 1,600 new voters were added to the rolls by January 1966. That month brought the death of Sammy Younge, a martyr to the civil rights movement. Younge, a Tuskegee Institute student from the local area, had become active in SNCC. Apparently, he had gone to a local gas station and gotten into a verbal conflict with the manager, Marvin Segrest, over the use of the bathroom. Ultimately, Younge was shot by Segrest and the campus erupted with marches and demands by the students. Tuskegee Institute President Luther Foster, who tried to calm the students, was unable to halt the demonstrations, which included a sit-down strike in the town square by 1,000 students led by Gwen Patterson. Another demonstration a week later resulted in the throwing of rocks and bottles when a deputy sheriff attempted to arrest one of the students.[38]

The TCA and liberal whites were appalled by the student behavior. When the next election approached, the split between the older blacks and the students was reflected in the candidates and the campaigning. The NPVL supported Thomas Reed for the state house of representatives, Arthur Scavella for Frances Rush's board of education position, and Lucius Amerson for sheriff. The TCA supported Jessie Guzman for the state legislature and Frances Rush for board of education but declined to endorse either candidate for sheriff. Amerson won 53 percent of the votes for sheriff, becoming the first black sheriff in Macon County. Reed and Scavella lost their races, but Reed and Attorney Fred Gray later were elected to the legislature (1970), the first black representatives from Macon County. That same year, Lurleen Wallace was elected to the governorship under her husband's tutelage. She appointed white "constables" in an effort to undermine Sheriff Amerson's authority, but most white Macon Countians accepted Amerson.[39]

In December 1966, Marvin Segrest went to trial in Opelika with an all-white jury for the murder of Sammy Younge. Predictably, he was acquitted. Just as predictably, 1,500 students marched to the downtown area where they defaced a Confederate statue in the square, broke into a liquor store, and threw rocks and bottles at store windows. Students again protested in 1967 when an interracial jury "failed to convict" a white man accused of raping a sixteen-year-old black girl. By 1968, students were protesting the war in Vietnam. When Dr. Martin Luther King Jr. was assassinated in April of that year, more protests were held; this time the students held the Tuskegee Institute Board of Directors hostage for thirteen hours to discuss their demands, forcing the temporary closing of the college.

At Tuskegee High School, the black enrollment had grown to more than 50 percent by the fall of 1966. Within the next two years, all white students withdrew, this time for good. Notasulga High School was the only integrated school in the county, probably because whites remained in the majority there.

Meanwhile, the splits in the black community became deeper—young vs. old, the college vs. the town, the lower class vs. the middle class, the rural areas vs. Tuskegee, the proponents of outright black control vs. the proponents of shared responsibility, and the NPVL vs. TCA. In this atmosphere, a teacher from Tysonville community in west Macon County, Consuelo "Connie" Harper, launched a challenge against the Macon County Community Action (MCCA) program. She said that the agency was not doing enough for the county's poor people. She wanted to found a Head Start program in her area and went over the heads of the MCCA to get funds directly from Washington. Harper's criticisms ultimately resulted in the dismissal of agency head, Beulah Johnson.[40]

About the same time, rural blacks led by Harper began to criticize the board of education for favoring Tuskegee over the rest of the county in policies and budgeting. Superintendent Wilson promised to equalize teacher-pupil ratios. His actions tended to put the onus for the problems on the middle-class blacks instead of the white-controlled system that had created the conditions in rural schools. In 1969, Charles Gomillion resigned from the school board when criticisms were leveled that white teachers and students who remained in the system were being treated with favoritism. The following year, 1970, the elections sent four blacks to the school board: Consuelo Harper, Dr. Ellis Hall, Dr. J. M. Henderson, and Dr. P. K. Biswas. They joined Frances Rush to form the first black-majority school board. Blacks also won other significant leadership positions: Lucius Amerson remained sheriff, Johnny L. Ford was elected mayor, Thomas Reed and Fred Gray were elected to the Alabama House of Representatives, and James Hopkins, who promised to remove all white employees if elected, was made circuit county clerk. Tuskegee and Macon County were now firmly in the hands of black leadership. It was a new and exciting experience.[41]

Dr. Joe Wilson resigned the superintendency following an altercation with Shorter community activist Connie Harper, so the school board went about searching for a new leader. During the interim, the principal of Tuskegee Institute High School, Alonzo Harvey, held the position.

A Note about the Introduction

This chapter is largely a summation of the work presented in the book *Reaping the Whirlwind: The Civil Rights Movement in Tuskegee,* by Robert J. Norrell. This book is thoroughly researched in primary sources, and no other source was found. I have chosen to use this book rather than spend arduous hours researching since the subject of our book concerns the period following most of these events. On the other hand, the reader who is unfamiliar with the Tuskegee story and milieu may not find Byas's story and his part in the ensuing drama as exciting and earth moving as it is.

CHAPTER 1
Early Life

My name is Ulysses Byas. On July 1, 1970, I became the first black public county school superintendent in Macon County (Tuskegee), Alabama, and the first in the entire Southeast.[1] I was an outsider stepping into a school system facing problems, most the result of centuries of neglect and segregation. But, as I said in 1970, "I knew there were problems here. People don't employ you unless there are problems."[2]

Many local citizens considered me an outsider, but being an outsider was nothing new to me. I've been an outsider all my life. After all, being black in America makes me a permanent outsider from some people's viewpoint. As I told a reporter in 1970, "I am aware that the spotlight will be on any negative thing that I might do."[3] Fortunately, my background had prepared me well for the challenges that I was to face.

Born in Macon, Georgia, on June 23, 1924, I was the second child and second son of Marie Smith Byas. She was nineteen years old at the time of my birth. From early 1926 until late 1935 (from the time I was two until the age of about twelve), Mother gave birth to four more children: my sister (who was her third child) and three more brothers. From shortly after his birth, my older brother lived across town with our grandparents. Consequently, for most of the time until age twelve, I was the eldest male living in the home. I do not remember my father, Eugene Byas, living in our home. In fact, growing up, I never knew his name. And if I had seen him, I would not have known he was my father. I was nearly twelve before I

1

learned his name while applying for a copy of my birth certificate. The topic was never discussed in our home.

Mother was married to Edward Sharpe in 1937. He was a good man and helpmate to my mother. They had two children: a boy and a girl.

Our home from my birth until 1935 was an unbroken, single-parent one. It was headed by a mother who, when necessary, served as mother and father to me and all of the children. And at times, especially with me, all of her mother/father skills were required just to keep me pointed in the right direction. She found ways to direct and redirect and keep me on course, even when I did not want to go her way. Believe me: I continue to lift my heart in gratitude to her, for all I am and hope to be. Furthermore, I give thanks and glory to God for making my mother a strong and determined woman who really believed that, regardless of the conditions, with God's help and by her own effort, she could work things out. She believed that with her heart and soul because of the pride she took in her children and her hope that we all would achieve worthwhile goals in life.

For about seven years, Mother worked as a domestic in the homes of various white families. During this time, she worked five and one-half days a week for seven hours or until she finished all the work assigned for that day. She was paid $2.50 per week; however, most families also let her bring home all the cooked food that was not eaten by the family. Often, she also did washing and ironing at home to supplement her meager income. The money earned doing laundry ranged from fifty to seventy-five cents per week. Thus, her income from both sources totaled at most $3.25 weekly.

For the remaining three years, Mother worked as a cook in a commercial establishment for six eight-hour days for a salary of $3.00 to $3.75 per week. Since she still managed to do laundry during this time, her total income rose to the lordly maximum of $4.50.

Two big expenditures had to come out of this income: rent, which averaged one dollar a week, and insurance premiums of forty cents per week, leaving the remainder for food, clothing, and all other household expenses. Throughout this period, we received assistance with food, clothing, and sometimes toys from governmental agencies and from civic clubs and churches, which were indispensable to our continued health and well-being. Another source of help was the school's soup program at two cents per bowl, which turned into the free and reduced lunch program. Later came the very welcome federal food-stamp program and the state's free textbook program, which supplemented our very inadequate household income.

During this period (1926–1935), no one in my house owned a toothbrush. In fact, upon entering the United States Navy in July 1943, my teeth were greenish-yellow. The navy doctor who examined me ordered me to purchase a toothbrush, my first ever. There were no washcloths in our house either. We had what we called a washrag, which was community property and, as such, was used by all—when we could find it! Most of the time, we had only one hair comb in the house as well. Near the end of this period, my three younger brothers and I slept in the same bed. Our sister usually slept in bed with Mother. At one time, for a short while, we all lived in a one-room apartment with an open fireplace. When our sister took a bath, all five boys had to go outside. Moreover, cooking, heating, bathing, and everything else were done in that room. And to make matters more difficult, we had to go across the street to get water from a faucet located in the yard of another house. For a bathroom, we used an outhouse.

We lived in eight or nine different rental houses of three rooms or less during this time. None of the houses, called shotgun houses, had inside running water (not even cold water), inside toilets or bathrooms, or electricity. Of course, there was no radio, and television was not yet known. Cooking was done on either a four-eye iron stove with an oven, on a two-eye hot plate, or even over an open fireplace, depending on the accommodations.

Water for drinking, cooking, and bathing invariably came from a communal faucet located in the yard. Many times during extremely cold winter nights, the faucet and the water we brought into the house would be frozen in the morning. On many such cold nights, we used the floor rug as an extra blanket on the bed to keep us warm as we slept. The community toilet was a hole in the ground, and it was enclosed in a wooden structure located at the far end of the backyard. The fear of rats and other rodents, as well as the cold winter weather, made it prohibitive to use the toilet after dark. Inside the house, lighting was obtained from a single kerosene lantern that was used primarily while getting ready for bed. School homework had to be done before nightfall, because we could not afford the luxury of burning the oil for any activity that could be done during the daylight.

If someone became ill, Mother always had a remedy for the ailment that excluded going to or calling the doctor. In fact, whenever we saw a medical doctor in the neighborhood, we asked, "Who's dead?"

Except for a Bible, there were no books in the house. I made the first radio, a crystal set, and first bicycle from pieces of broken items I found. Needless to say, life was hard since much of my childhood occurred during the Great Depression. Of course, we shared the misery with millions of other people. We were poor. But as my mother always reminded us, there is poor, and there is poor in spirit. We were poor, but we were never poor in spirit!

As the oldest child at home for most of my childhood, I wanted to be a help to my mother. I was less than four years old when I first heard her singing late at night.

> If the world from you withhold its silver and its gold,
> And you have to get along with meager fare,
> Just remember in His Word, how He feeds the little bird,
> Take your burden to the Lord and leave it there.
>
> When your enemies assail and your heart begins to fail,
> Don't forget that God in heaven answers prayer. He will make a
> way for you and lead you safely through.
> Take your burden to the Lord and leave it there.[4]

One day after her fourth child was born, Mother was in bed and called to me. She said that she wanted some water. No water was in the house, and the four-foot-high faucet was located in the backyard. I told her I would get some water for her, and she replied, "You can't reach the faucet. It is too high for you." I believed then and thereafter that I could do whatever needed to be done, for there is truth in the saying "Where there is a will, there is a way."

4

"Be careful," Mother cautioned. I went into the creek running at the side of the house and got bricks and rocks. I used them to build a mound to stand upon so I could reach the faucet. Oh, what a joy I felt when she got the pail of water, and I saw her grateful reaction. I will never forget her remark. "You are so smart! I am very proud of you." From that day on, my only desire was to be helpful to her.

When I earned money, I would give it to my mother. Some of the things I did to earn pennies were bringing coal and wood into the house for nearby neighbors. Some would also give me food. I would walk through fields, streets, and vacant houses looking for nails, scrap iron, bottles, rags, and anything else the junkman would buy. Sometimes, I located a field of grass to which I drove a neighbor lady's cow for grazing.

As my world grew larger, I sold special editions of the local newspaper and Sunday editions of the regional papers. In addition, I sold weekly editions of the national black newspapers. While in upper elementary school, I got a job cleaning in a downtown company that made candy. They paid me a dime a day and gave me a sack filled with scrap candy, rings, and trinkets, which I sold to classmates. At times on Saturdays and during the summers, I would go with my uncle on an ice wagon drawn by two mules to take twenty-five- and fifty-pound blocks of ice into homes. Once, after Mother learned that I was carrying the fifty-pound blocks of ice, she told her brother that she didn't want me to pick up anything that heavy. So whenever he got an order for that amount, he would say, "Marie don't want you to pick up this much ice." He would pick it up and put it on my shoulder and say, "Hurry back." While in high school, I held two jobs downtown. One was as a bicycle delivery boy at a sandwich shop and the other was as a shoeshine and hat-cleaning boy. My last two years in high school, I got up at 2:30 in the morning, walked or rode my bicycle four miles , and then walked five miles while delivering 150 newspapers.

Other jobs which I held prior to entering the teaching profession were cutting grass, garbage pickup, assisting a man who bought scrap iron and bottles, carpenter's helper, apprentice carpenter, carpenter, cook, stage carpenter, lay machine operator, and painter. Whatever the job, I always tried to do my very best in pleasing my employer.

When I was in upper elementary, or what is called middle school today, I began to see the world as much wider than our very poor neighborhood where everyone was struggling to survive. I saw that our economic situation was grave, and I wanted to quit school and get a job so that I could better contribute to the family's well-being. I started badgering Mother to quit school, but she wouldn't hear of it. She told me I was going to stay in school and graduate.

Finally, when I got to eighth grade, she said to me, "Since you think you're grown, you're going to get a job and give me half of everything you earn." I already had a job promised as a bicycle delivery boy at $4.50 a week, working 8 a.m. to 10:30 p.m. every day but Sunday. Then I had to give Mother $2.25 of that. After about two months, I wanted to quit, but Mother said, "No, you've already messed up the school year, and you can't quit unless you have another job lined up." I realized then that she had won that battle, and when school started that next fall, I had already bought school supplies and hidden them under my bed. She never talked to me about going back to school again. I was waiting for her to say something about school, but she never did. I got up, got dressed, and she asked if I was going to work. I said, "No, I'm going to school." I had learned in two months that there were some things worse than going to school! We laughed about that when I graduated from Fort Valley State College. When I went off to graduate school, she said, "I used to have to call the police to get you to go to school, and now I'll have to call the police to get you to stop!"

It was and is still a source of inspiration to me to remember Mother's encouraging statements of hope for a better tomorrow. She never tired of saying to me, "I know you can." She said the same thing to each of her children. This attitude and the relationship she established among her children made many disadvantages easier to overcome. One such potential disadvantage was our limited and even inadequate amount of financial resources. However, our self-confidence and working together to achieve common objectives made all of us know that the lack of things could not, and would not, be a barrier to a successful future. I am certain that Mother read and understood Psalm 40:17 and knew the Lord would come on His own schedule. I base my belief in this matter upon the many times I heard her singing various verses of the song "Leave It There." The verse which reads, "But I am poor and needy; yet the Lord thinketh upon me; thou art my help and my deliverer; make no tarrying, O my God," makes it clear to me, in retrospect, that Mother knew there was a law of compensation which assured that the honest and just person would not suffer long. Moreover, I felt that she possessed that priceless, multifaceted attribute of an infectiously brave, hardworking, honest pride in her children, and the courageous ability to pursue her goals, despite the people who told her that those goals were unattainable under her times and circumstances.

Neither they nor my mother knew that, for about half of those critical years, the business tide of economic prosperity was at full flood and that the latter half would be swept up in the depths of Depression. Yet both the Roaring Twenties and the Great Depression were times when Mother and many of our acquaintances were being socially ostracized and economically swindled, and most of the victims harbored no expectations of a better tomorrow. At the same time, we and others were living at a level some consider subhuman. If Mother ever read Shakespeare's *Hamlet*, I am not aware of it. Nevertheless, her thinking was consistent with the bard's following lines:

> My will, Not all the world
> And for my means, I'll husband them so well
> They shall go far with little.[5]

Inclusive among her "means" was her future-thinking ability, which allowed her to grasp opportunities each day to see just what the future would offer her children. She wanted me and each of my siblings to be prepared to take advantage of whatever high school graduation offered. Therefore, she sacrificed to ensure that we each had the chance to complete public school education rather than allowing us to drop out and start earning a living, even though that would have been easier for her.

I'm sometimes asked where I got my values from, particularly as relates to integrity. Mother is responsible for that too. When we were kids, we did a lot of working, selling newspapers or candy, whatever, and sometimes we would come home with something of value: an old ball or some wire, for example. Well, Mother would ask so many questions about where we got the item. One was this: "Was it out in a ditch or was it is somebody's yard?" When she finished asking questions, we were sorry we'd found the darn thing. I made our first bicycle out of scrap parts that I had found, and I had to go through a grilling every time I came home with a spoke. She didn't have anything to do with anybody stealing things.

One day following such an inquisition, she told a story I've never forgotten. She said that a man she knew worked in a downtown shoe store, he had a pair of shoes for sale, and she bought them from him. A few days later, she was walking in the downtown area when she looked up to see she was by that same shoe store. There was a man standing in front of the store and he seemed to be looking hard at her shoes, so she jumped into an alley, took the shoes off, threw them in the garbage, and walked home without any shoes at all. When we were younger, we didn't understand how powerful that lesson had been for her, but we saw that she chased anyone away if they came around to the house selling anything that was "hot."

Some people may consider our family an incomplete social unit, but I beg to strongly disagree with them. My family was not the traditional nuclear family, to be sure. It was headed for more than ten years by Mother and was unbroken; we each were accepted as persons and we felt extreme pleasure in being helpful to the rest of the family. Each of us was given positions of household responsibility throughout our childhood years. This strategy enabled us, as we reached adulthood, to assume adult citizenship responsibilities.

When Mother was in elementary school, between the years 1911 and 1916, she often went with her mother, my grandmother, to a domestic job in the home of a white family with several daughters. We surmise that the daughters often talked, in Mother's presence, about their high school activities and the kinds of positions they expected to enter upon graduation. It was apparently during this time that she began to think seriously about her own entry into high school, about graduating, and about later getting a good-paying position. With eager anticipation, she looked forward to her high school career, so it was a massive disappointment that faced her when she learned, upon finishing the seventh grade, that her public school system (in Bibb County, Georgia) offered high school only to white students. She had reached the end of her road in education simply based on the color of her skin. This outright discrimination hurt her deeply and, had she had the opportunity to read Henry Adams, she would undoubtedly have agreed with him that high school graduation should lessen the obstacles, diminish the friction, invigorate the energy, and should train the mind to react, not in haphazard, but by choice, on the lines of force that attract their world.[6]

Yes! She was a very strong woman and an even stronger mother. She believed in Christianity and the hope it offered for a better and greater day coming, even when she felt cheated and discriminated against because of her race. She probably found relief in the words of Paul to the Romans (12:12). "Rejoicing in hope, patient in tribulation, continuing instant in prayer."

Shortly after my birth, the school system opened a public high school for blacks in Macon. When the high school opened, Mother was expecting her third child, and she often expressed the feeling that the Lord Himself had made it possible for her children to finish high school, although she had not. From that time forward, this became her vision and constant sermon. She would say, "I want my children to finish high school." Persistently and with emotion, she articulated this idea to me and to my brothers and sister, both individually and collectively. When we entered first grade, the end objective was to finish high school. As a companion to her vision and sermon, it was her belief that she could, with precise accuracy, determine which of her children were smart and quick learners and which were not as smart or were slow learners. She constantly shared her conclusions with each of us along with the reiteration of her vision. "I want *all* my children to finish high school." She expected the smart and quick learners to make passing grades at all times. The less smart and slower to learn could take more time, if needed, but in the end, all were expected to pass all courses.

Mother concluded that I was one of the smart and quick learners, and as such, she expected me to earn passing grades in all subjects. Yet school did not come easily for me. My second grade teacher beat me so severely that Mother took me out of school for the remainder of that school year.

After working a number of odd jobs while my siblings were in school, I was ready to return to school. Once again, after starting at Hudson High School, I dropped out in the eighth grade and went to work as a bicycle delivery boy for a drugstore. I worked fourteen hours a day, six days a week, for $4.50 per week. I

9

realized that I wanted more, so I returned to high school. Then in my junior year, at the age of seventeen, I attempted to join the army. Mother unwillingly signed the papers, and I went for my physical. The doctors turned me down, stating that I had tuberculosis. When I returned home, Mother took me to a doctor for treatment, but he did not find any tuberculosis! So I resumed my studies and, because I was eighteen, my name came up in the draft during my senior year. The draft board granted me a deferment to complete high school since I was only a few months from graduation. I graduated in 1943, smack in the middle of World War II, and the draft board sent me to the navy.

Having completed high school, I entered the United States Navy and served as a cook's helper for the duration of the war. Black sailors were never taught how to swim, and we never had an opportunity for advancement in the highly segregated navy. Despite my high school diploma and the achievement of Mother's dream, I was an outsider on the inside of the ship!

The navy used to have propaganda sessions where officers told us about the racist Hitler and why we were fighting. I just listened, but my mind told me that Hitler hadn't done anything to me but the American racists here certainly had! When I first volunteered for the army, I was told that I had tuberculosis and that I couldn't join. Mother took me to a doctor who said he could find no evidence of tuberculosis. So our meager resources were wasted, and I returned to finish high school. Meanwhile, blacks were being criticized as unpatriotic for not joining up.

So following graduation, I got into the navy. The navy had what it called *The Bluejacket's Manual*, with all the rules and regulations in it. The officers were supposed to conduct an "abandon ship" drill, but I was never given such instruction, because I was never stationed where they had facilities for blacks. Likewise, we never got swimming instructions, because there was no swimming pool for blacks. Some blacks who wanted to swim would slip over to the whites' swimming pool at midnight!

According to *The Blue Jacket Manual*, the navy policy was to assign sailors to the post where they were best suited. And a personnel specialist came around to examine the records and reassign sailors. Several of my friends were examined and transferred to other divisions, although none of these fellows were high school graduates. But I was never called for examination. I had already served more than two years in the navy and I was puzzled, so *The Blue Jacket Manual* said I could look at my personnel records during normal working hours. When I went to check my records, the clerk told me I couldn't see them, so I told them I would write to the secretary of the navy and the president and anybody else I could think of since I was denied a right spelled out in the manual. Then the clerk told me to go to the captain on the base and get permission to see my records, so I headed to his office, which was across the base and upstairs. The officer may have thought I wouldn't go to the captain, but he called the secretary to the captain and told him that if I showed up to send me back because he had found my records.

Consequently, I got to see my records, because I was determined to follow all the procedures to gain my rights, and I saw immediately why I was not being promoted. Somebody had written on my record that I had dropped out of school in the ninth grade!

Nevertheless, and despite my perceived meager educational background, in the first seven months in the navy I had risen to the rank of cook third class, a rank that is equivalent to a staff sergeant in the army. I suppose they thought I had gone as far as it was possible with my limited education!

Here's another way racism and favoritism prevented me from advancing. Theoretically, we trained in the use of side arms, so when a flight finished training, they not only transferred the flight, they also transferred the support group (cooks, stewards, etc.). The only way to keep a support group from transferring with their flight was to declare them "essential to the operation of the base." Here I was a cook and they kept transferring me to another incoming flight instead of moving me with my group. That happened four or five times, and it kept me in the mess branch instead of using me where I was "best suited."

I didn't like this process at all, but we were trained to always say, "Yes, sir," and I learned how to say a nasty, "Yes, sir," when an officer upset me, using facial expressions and body gyrations, but he couldn't do a thing about it as long as I said, "Yes, sir." I've always been a person who believed that you may not be able to do anything about being mistreated, but I could surely let the mistreater know that I was aware of the mistreatment and was not satisfied with it.

Taking advantage of the GI Bill, I went to college when I completed my service with the navy. At Fort Valley State College (now a university), I studied teaching and industrial arts, graduating in 1950. Fort Valley was created from the federal land-grant program exclusively for blacks because the University of Georgia, the other land-grant college, was solely for whites. Thanks to some wise and dedicated educators, such as Dr. C. V. Troup, Fort Valley offered an excellent and nurturing experience for us. From there, I went to Columbia University in New York, where I completed a master's degree in educational administration.

As a teacher, I worked with both children and adults, in both academics and industrial arts, starting at Douglasville, Georgia, and rising quickly to the position of supervising principal. One time, the second year I was principal in north Georgia, I made a decision to change class ring companies. Principals used to decide which company would provide the class rings and other memorabilia for students. When I went there, a controversy was raging about whether company A or company B should be the vendor. That first year, I told both salesmen that I would check with my predecessor for that year but that I would make my own decision the following year. So the second year came and I decided to use Herff Jones, who had hired a black representative. The other company's representative said to me, "That's the trouble now with all this integration!" It was about 1954 and this white man went to the long-standing chairman of the board of education and told him that I was an integrationist. That was supposed to be the kiss of death for a black principal. Soon, I noticed that influential whites, who had never talked to me previously, were talking with me and asking questions. I thought, *These folks are trying you out; you'd better answer these questions right.* And apparently, I did. Next fall, this salesman was so sure I had been replaced that he came back to the school, and with the exterior door open, he could see straight up the hall and into my office. When he saw me there, he turned around and never reappeared.

Another incident that occurred while I was principal had to do with integration. The General Assembly had created a committee that visited the various congressional districts to discuss whether or not we were going to desegregate our public schools. Before the committee reached our district, my superintendent came to me and asked me what my folks wanted. Then he said they were getting up a petition against desegregation and he wanted me to get blacks to sign it. He also said he wanted me to testify. One of my colleagues in the principalship called me and wanted to know whether I was going to attend the hearing, and I said that I wasn't going. He replied that his man was putting pressure on him to attend, and I said that my man was putting on pressure too, but I wasn't accepting it. This colleague went to the committee hearing, and by the end of the year, his own folks had chased him out of the school district.

How did I avoid testifying? This is what I said to the superintendent: "Mr. Blakely, as far as I'm concerned, you and the board of education always make the decisions about who is going to attend which schools. You have never conversed with me about these decisions, and I didn't worry about it then or now. I just accept whomever you send me, and my job is to coordinate and create the best program I can for those students and teachers under the circumstances I'm given. If it's all right with you, I'd rather leave that problem with you."

He didn't bother me anymore after that.

By 1968, I had been principal of E. E. Butler Junior and Senior High School in Gainesville, Georgia, for eleven years, was serving as president of the Georgia Teachers and Education Association (GTEA), and had been widely hailed for my leadership and innovative programs,[7] when the school board finally decided to integrate the high schools of Gainesville. At that time, the superintendent offered me a "position within the administration" rather than the principalship of the integrated high school. I knew I was still the outsider. I had earned the principalship by my work at Butler. I did not want a made-up position with no authority. So, to the amazement and disappointment of many, I resigned from the school system, which meant uprooting my wife and family of four children to move somewhere else.

I took a position as assistant executive secretary of the GTEA, the National Education Association's affiliate for black educators who had been kept out of the Georgia Education Association (GEA) until very recently. GTEA had its headquarters in Atlanta, so that's where I headed.

While working at GTEA, we conducted research to discover what had happened to black educators as school systems were forced to desegregate. We discovered that my story was a common one. Most of the black educational leaders (principals, coaches, etc.) and many of the classroom teachers had been displaced and whites were given their jobs when the schools in their community integrated. We published the results of this study in the *GTEA Herald,* our association publication.

One of my duties at GTEA was negotiating with GEA about the merger of our two associations, as required by the NEA. We were determined to make the merger as fair as possible to our members and staff. We insisted on shared power and alternating presidencies (black and white) for the first few years of union. The merger was accomplished in April 1970, at which time I became the director of administration and special services of a new organization called the Georgia Association of Educators (GAE). It was only a few months later that I again shocked many people by accepting the position as superintendent of Macon County (Alabama) Schools at a salary much below what I was making at GAE. As I explained to my friend and former boss, Dr. Horace Tate, I wanted to go as high as I could, and the only position higher than principal was superintendent of a school system.

CHAPTER 2
First Things First

Macon County had elected its first majority black school board and it needed a new superintendent. Evidently, leaders contacted the area universities for recommendations, which is how I became involved. I had a good relationship with Auburn University's dean of the School of Education, Truman Pierce, whom I met through the Southeastern Education Laboratory (SEL). The US government funded education laboratories across the country, and the one that was funded in our area encompassed the tristate area of Georgia, Alabama, and Florida. Its purpose was to eliminate educational deprivation in the tristate area. The bylaws specified that the members of the board of directors would be the deans of schools of education, including Tuskegee Institute, University of Alabama, Auburn University, University of Florida, Florida State University, University of Georgia, and Emory University. And the bylaws also spelled out that the president of the state high school principals association would be a member of the board of directors. I was then the president of the all-black high school principals association in Georgia. So I became a member of the board of directors among all these college deans.

We used to have some heated discussions, because when the deans came up with things they wanted to do, I said, "You all talk like you're dealing with the most significant problems connected with educational deprivation. You all don't see the worst problems, because we cull that out before we come to you. So you all have got to understand that the major problem of educational deprivation is among people you don't ever see, and you all always want to spend your money on programs of that deprivation that you see, but that's not the real deprivation." We used to have heated dialogues, and invariably, I was on one side and everybody else was on the other side. But I established a good rapport with the other members, and the deans, for the most part, were favorably impressed with my ideas and my ability to articulate why I had such beliefs.

So when Macon County (Alabama) was looking for a new superintendent, the dean of the School of Education in Tuskegee, Dean Hunter, was approached by the members of the Macon County Board of Education to recommend somebody, and he recommended me. The board members asked me to send my references to them, so I did, and I included the name of my last superintendent in Gainesville. Apparently, he didn't give me a good recommendation, because the board representative called me and said, "You've got to send some more references." He said, "Don't use your last superintendent." I surmised that he must have said a lot of negative things about me. We had parted company in a negative way. Whenever I disagreed with Blakeney Revis, I'd always tell him. It didn't make any change in his actions, but it gave me ease over it. I said, "When people do something negative against me, I may not be able to change it, but I can let them know that I'm not pleased with it. I'm dissatisfied." So when Revis told me that he was going to merge the black high school with the white high school, he added, "When I do, confidentially, I'm going to recommend you to be assistant superintendent."

I said, "The hell you are. I'm the best high school principal in Georgia, and I know I'm the best in this state."

Revis said, "Well, Mr. Byas, I can't understand you. I'm talking about a promotion for you, and you acting like that."

I said, "Promotion is what the worker thinks, and that's your idea of a promotion, not mine. I only hear you saying that I'll not be considered as the principal of the new high school." I continued. "I've got a choice right now: I can choose to stay here next year as principal or I can choose to leave. But if I choose to stay, then you're telling me that I won't have that choice. So I'm going to leave while I have a choice."

Revis got upset. He had to do a lot of explaining to the community regarding why he couldn't find something acceptable to keep me in Gainesville, because I was doing a whole lot of community work. So I think that's why he didn't give me a good recommendation for the Macon County job.

Initially, I had not asked Truman Pierce, dean of the School of Education in Auburn, for a recommendation. Nor had I asked Clyde Blair, Alabama's assistant superintendent in charge of curriculum, who was also on the SEL board of directors, so I called Blair and told him I was a candidate and I needed a recommendation. "Oh, Mr. Byas, you're the man for the job. I'll call right now, and I'll follow it with a letter."

Truman Pierce said the same thing. Of course, Dean Hunter had already recommended me. Then I went to my brag book, where I had three or four letters that my former superintendent had written in appreciation for some outstanding job that I had done. I reproduced copies of those and sent them to the committee. Once I did all that, the opposition died down.

My appointment so upset my former superintendent that when I went to a national meeting the following year, I looked up and Revis was coming my way. He saw me and turned and went the other way. I cut him off. I said, "Hey, man, you look like you try to dodge me." He wasn't happy to see me!

I guess he wasn't the only one who was upset. The board that selected me had four blacks and one white female who was the chairman of the board, a lady by the name of Frances Rush. She had to write me a letter telling me that the board had named me the superintendent of schools, and then she *rushed* right out the school district! I never had a chance to work with her. She resigned from the school board and left, which doesn't surprise me, because historically during desegregation, the so-called white liberals would cooperate with blacks so long as they were electing a white to the position. But the white cooperation stopped when it came to trying to elect blacks to the position. So she was working well with the blacks until the majority of blacks decided they wanted a black superintendent. I told somebody when I learned that Ms. Rush had resigned, "Well, she's true to her name." She rushed on out, eventually sold the house, and moved out of the county.

Unfortunately, there were negative attitudes among some of the people in the county too. When the word got out that the board had employed a new superintendent from Georgia, and from Atlanta, some people in one area spread the rumor that the board had hired a Black Panther. In another area, somebody said it had hired a white person because nobody had seen me.

I went to Tuskegee at the invitation of the board during the daytime for an appointment on the campus, and that's where they interviewed me. When we completed the interview, I decided that if they hired me, I would take the job without visiting the schools or looking at the problems. It was the best decision I ever made, because had I looked at the problems, there's no way in hell I'd have left my job in Atlanta to go there!

Well, when the board announced my coming, I got a telegram. One board member called me and told there had been mass meetings and some protesters decided to send me a telegram that basically told me the citizens were interested in somebody else, and that in the interests of public education in the county, the best contribution I could make would be to withdraw my name. The telegram said that all of the bus drivers, all of the teacher aides, all of the teachers, and all of the principals were against my coming. So the board members called me. They were concerned and upset about it. And I said to the board, "Well, I interpreted the telegram as being *pro* somebody else not *anti* me. Couldn't be *anti* me," I said, "because they don't know me." And that was a good stance to take, because after about four months there, the person who took the initiative of sending the telegram asked for an appointment with me. She came in the office. She said a lot of things, but to sum it up, she said, "We really didn't know. You're the best thing to happen to schools in Macon County."

That was Wilhelmina Baldwin. Wilhelmina had been in the district for over twenty-five years; she had been principal of a little school when they had 400 to 500 different schools in the county. She moved from one place to the other. She later became my director of curriculum and instruction. Wilhelmina became one of my best supporters.

Another person who got to be my good supporter was Connie Harper. She was the person who had been responsible for the board having released my white predecessor from his position. Community members were picketing and protesting in front of his office. She was carrying a placard and said he hit her. (Later, she said he hadn't hit her but he had brushed up beside the placard.) However, when that came up, the folks just got all upset with Mr. Wilson, and they ran him out of the county.

MACON COUNTY BOARD OF EDUCATION

Mr. Allen Adams, Tuskegee Community, is married and has two children. He is a local businessman.

Dr. P. K. Biswas, Chairman, Tuskegee Community, is married and has one child. He is a faculty member at Tuskegee Institute and a local businessman.

Dr. Ellis Hall, Tuskegee Institute Community, is married and has six children. He is Director of Clinics of the School of Veterinary Medicine, Tuskegee Institute and a local businessman.

Mrs. Consuella Harper, Shorter Community, is married and has two children. She is the Director of OIC Montgomery, Alabama.

Dr. J. H. M. Henderson, Vice-Chairman, Tuskegee Institute Community, is married and has four children. He is Director of the Carver Research Foundation at Tuskegee Institute and a local businessman.

Ms. Harper was appointed to fill a vacancy on the school board created when, just prior to my coming, a white reverend had resigned. Connie was one who really believed the superintendent should have been an Alabaman, at the least. To go outside the district was bad enough, but then to go outside Alabama was unforgivable, as far as she was concerned, and she was really critical at board meetings. After about eight months, the board was meeting at Shorter, and Mrs. Harper asked for a point of personal privilege. And she started off, I never shall forget her words, "Members of the board, people present, our new superintendent, I've been watching him ever since he's been here." I said to myself, "Ain't that the damn truth." And she said some other things, but she ended with, "You know I want to be the first to say he's been good for the school system. He's brought a lot of good things here. We're fortunate to have him. And I think the board ought to draw up a resolution of commendation. And I'd like to be on the committee to do it."

So the board voted then and there for a resolution of commendation. Eventually, two board members wrote it up. A couple of years later, they gave me another commendation.

All those people who took the leadership in sending the negative telegram became my strongest supporters. I started believing that most people, when given a free choice to go with who they know—even though they have faults—or to go with somebody that they know nothing about, will choose to go with the person they know. Believing that, I said if I have anything on the ball that I could win those folks over. And Wilhelmina Baldwin was one of the first. But I had no animosity toward the writers of that telegram, because I didn't even open it until years after I had left Tuskegee! A board member had told that the telegram would be coming, so when it came, I put in the file unopened. I think I was in New York before I opened that telegram and read it. Likewise, when some of the other critics that I knew to be hell-raisers sent me letters complaining about something, I didn't open them either! If it said, "Addressee only," or something like that, it stayed in the envelope until I moved away.

One very small contingent of naysayers supported Alonzo Harvey, the principal at TIHS, who had served as the acting superintendent in the interim between Mr. Wilson and me. One gal who was the main leader of the group courted him. I didn't hold any animosity against them. Now, a leader who does not get cooperation can't do his job! My job as a leader is to get the cooperation from folks who want to cooperate, folks who don't want to cooperate, and folks who pretend that they'll cooperate but are insincere. It's my obligation to get cooperation. I got cooperation from everybody. I had to work harder to get it from some than from others, and some reluctantly saw that if they didn't show a certain measure of cooperation, it would be self-defeating. Some people don't have the capacity to make the necessary changes; with those people, the leader has got to help them see that cooperating may be in their best interest. But whatever the reasons, some people wanted to cooperate and some people didn't. I didn't have any complaints about cooperation. There were a few diehards who never got over the fact that they didn't name Mr. Harvey as superintendent, but they were misguided. One of the persons in that group approached me several times, about what I did when I went to these cities to attend big meetings, and she wanted me to carry her with me when I went to these big hotels. But I never did fall for any stuff like that. So that may have been why she was against me.

When I came to Tuskegee in July 1970, I faced several immediate problems: the deplorable condition of the buildings, the financial crisis, and the court order to desegregate the faculties of the schools. Then there was the long-term need for curriculum improvement and improvement in student achievement.

The desegregation of the faculties was perhaps the easiest problem to solve, and it may have been an advantage that I was an outsider. You see, I had my staff draw up a list of names with positions, race, and other demographic information. Then, without knowing anyone personally, I assigned them so that each school had an equal proportion of black and white teachers. Nobody could accuse me of favoritism, and the transfers were accomplished with little commotion.

The next problem I tackled was the desperate financial situation. Well, when you're strapped for cash and you're running a deficit, you have to first examine those areas in which you're spending even limited funds, and you place them in order of priority—the area where you're spending most of your money first. For Macon County Schools, that one area was in instructional supplies. We had been allocating money to local schools and each one would do its own buying; the prices they paid would vary. One school would pay $2.95 for a ream of paper and another school would pay $4.50. The larger schools would order two or three cases, and the smaller schools would order two or three reams at a time. Where you ordered two to three reams, you'd pay maybe two dollars more per ream. We saw an opportunity to save money in instructional supplies and even to provide more supplies to schools by doing central purchasing. To give an example, we were able to put out bids for carload lots of paper, and we got it for 58 cents a ream.

Furthermore, this process helped a local black businessman grow his company. He was the successful bidder for our school supplies the first year, but his suppliers wouldn't advance him credit because they said his credit line had been limited to $5,000. However, the supplier agreed that if the superintendent would agree that he would pay any invoice due as a result of that bid, by making the check out jointly to the local man and the wholesaler, that they would let him have the credit. We did it gladly. We got a carload lot of paper and other supplies. We set up central receiving and hired a paraprofessional to operate that department. And we saved a lot of money on that, plus we were able to do it without going out of paper before the next year. We were able to provide everybody with supplies to carry through the year.

However, the initial year, we had to suspend all purchases until January. Everybody had been ordering at the beginning of the school year. That was a problem because we didn't get our tax money until December and sometimes as late as January. Therefore, we had been spending money before we got it. Plus there was a deficit from the previous year. So that first year, we didn't order anything. We said, "We're going to wait until we get the tax money. Then we'll put in our orders after January." When we got the money, we went to the vendors and said we could pay them within thirty days and get an additional 30 percent discount. Of course, it hurt the schools that first year because they had been accustomed to getting supplies when school opened, but they had to go—from September through December—without school supplies. If they didn't have any left over from the previous spring, they had to get by the best way they could, but thereafter they were home free. Because we were doing central bidding, we saved money on that, and when we ordered in February or March, we got enough to carry over to the following school year. Once that process was in place, it worked beautifully. All of our instructional supplies were ordered centrally, as well as equipment like student desks and chairs, catalogued when they came in and delivered through our central warehouse. In addition to the savings from cost per item of the central warehousing and inventory control was the elimination of apparent theft of items that were alleged to be going to the segregation academy.

Clearly, there were big problems with school finance. It really surprised me how the citizens always talked about taxes. The taxpayers of Macon County, in comparison to what it cost us to operate the schools, paid us almost nothing. (See the charts on pages 103 and 106.) The basic support of the schools, what little bit we had, came from the state. And then—when soft money started being available from the federal government—we went all out for that. We had a successful record. Fortunately, I had built up a good reputation among the federal people. But the regular fiscal support was limited by state law.

The state constitution authorized the local board, with voter approval, to place either a five-mill tax or a three-mill tax, or a one-mill tax and later a special five-mill tax, and those taxes could be set up for a period of time ranging from fifteen to thirty years. And that had to be spelled out. For instance, if we wanted the special five-mill tax, we had to put that up for a vote of the citizens of the district. Say we wanted to levy a special five-mill tax for fifteen years. Once the voters approved, then for fifteen years we had that approval, but it expired at the end of fifteen years.

Now in school districts where they were doing a lot of building and the value in the property increased every year, they got increased earning from that tax. But in districts where the total assessed value of property was decreasing, then there would be a decrease. Since Tuskegee was losing businesses and residents due to white flight, a one-time special five-mill tax in Tuskegee brought in more money in the past than it was currently bringing in. Now most of the voter-approved taxes had been approved, as I recall, for twenty to thirty years. It had been so long ago that most of the citizens didn't even know that they had to vote for the school taxes. In the later part of 1975, maybe as late as 1976, our voter approval was expiring. So I had to lead a campaign to get the taxes approved for another period of time. And I had to explain it to citizens who didn't understand they were supposed to even vote for school taxes. Some of them had voted for everything except school taxes. Remember most blacks in Macon County only got the right to register and vote in the 1960s.

I had to go to all these units throughout the county and every little PTA meeting and try to explain state law and how we set the school taxes. And I had to get the voters to approve all of those local school taxes. When you start talking to a thirty-five-year-old parent to vote for a twenty-five-year-old tax, he was only ten years old when it was last passed—he didn't know anything about voting for school tax, whether he was black or white. And if he was a black citizen of any age, he couldn't have voted back then anyway. So I said to citizens, "If you don't approve the tax, this is how much money we'll lose." But that was revealing. They asked, "Do we supposed to vote on that?" We had to educate folks, and that problem fell on me as superintendent.

Besides supplies, we spent a lot of money on gasoline for buses. We operated more than 100 bus routes. We were using a huge number of gallons of gas and we had four gasoline depots. The wholesalers were delivering up to 1,000 gallons of gasoline at a time, and at the end of the month, we had a stack of delivery slips almost a foot thick. More importantly, nobody could document whether or not we actually received that gasoline. There came a time when I was convinced, in my own mind's eye, that part of the gasoline we were paying for never got to the school district. In fact, I thought we were paying for gasoline to operate the private school buses. But rather than to make that announcement to the board, which I knew would require a higher level of proof than what convinced me in my own mind's eye, and that would take precious time to document and possibly lead to a court case, I decided to go another route.

The idea and procedure that I sold the board was that it was not good business practice to be as dependent upon regular gasoline deliveries as we had been since we could only store a three-day supply. I argued that we ought to increase our storage capacity, so that we could have on hand at least a thirty-day supply of gasoline. We decided to increase our storage capacity so that we could accept, in one delivery, a tank car of gasoline, which is 10,000 gallons. At South Macon, we had a storage facility that could take a thousand gallons; D. C. Wolfe could take a thousand gallons; at Notasulga, we had storage for 500 gallons; and at the central office at Tuskegee, we had underground storage for 10,000 gallons. To solve this problem, we increased the central underground storage to 30,000 gallons by putting in two more 10,000-gallon underground tanks.

In 1972 when the gasoline shortage hit, the federal regulations stated that the wholesaler who had supplied us with gasoline in the previous year had to set aside at least that amount for the following year. However, none of our suppliers had gasoline all of a sudden, regardless of the regulations. I contacted Birmingham, the regional office in Atlanta, and even the Washington, DC, office, but nobody could get any gasoline for us. There came a morning when my gasoline supervisor called me and said he had pumped the last gallon of gas into the buses. I went a lot of places, called several major oil suppliers like Gulf, Standard Oil, and BP, and none of them had gasoline. Well, a retailer in Montgomery, a black retailer, said he'd let me have gas, but I had to transport it from his pump; he couldn't deliver it. He suggested where I could buy a used 500-gallon gasoline truck, so we bought it and pumped 500 gallons from his supply. That saved us for another day! Then my school attorney, who lived in Alexander City, got his local distributor to agree to sell us gas. But when the Alexander City distributor delivered the gas to us, the local distributors in Tuskegee heard about it and complained to the corporation. They threatened to cut him off if he continued delivering outside his own area, so that source dried up too.

In desperation that next morning, I told my secretary that I was going north on I-85, I didn't know where in the hell I was going, but I'd call her. And when I got twenty-five to thirty miles up I-85, I happened to look across at south 85 and saw a gasoline tanker going south. I crossed over and caught up with him. When he stopped to make a delivery, I went over to introduce myself, I told him my problem, and he suggested that I ought to try independent dealers. I told him I had called Gulf and Standard, and he said, "No, you need to try independent dealers."

When I went back to the office, we looked up independent gasoline dealers, and I called all the numbers but one that I had purposely ignored because the name of the company was obnoxious to me. The name of the company was Rebel Oil Company. Having gotten nowhere with the other companies, I finally decided, "I guess I'll call these damn rebels." So I asked my secretary to call Rebel Oil, and the owner got on the line. I gave the man the particulars of my problem. He said, "Well, let me call you back within ten minutes." I'm satisfied he wanted to verify whether my call was a hoax or legitimate. And sure enough, he called back. He didn't ask for me by name. He said to my secretary, "Let me speak to the superintendent." He asked, "What's his name?" and she told him. And then I got on the line. He told me, "Well, I've got a tank car with 10,000 gallons in it. We can have it over at your place by 9:30 tomorrow morning, but we have to make a one-drop delivery and here's what it costs. And before we unload, you have to give my man a cashier's check for that amount." I said, "We'll have it."

And when that tanker pulled in that next morning, all of those segregationists were shocked. Strangely enough, within twenty-four hours, the three local distributors had gasoline. So we were able to resolve that problem. And because we had capacity for 30,000 gallons, we were able to tell the suppliers when we wanted deliveries, and all of it came to our central office. Then we used our truck to deliver our own gas to the outer areas as needed. So we got the accountability system instituted, meaning that we effectively cut off the supply that was going outside the system, and the money we spent for gasoline went down.

Then we did another thing to save gasoline. On all of the buses, bus drivers basically determined where they were going to stop every morning and afternoon. So I came up with a plan, with the board's approval, whereby we would hire a high school student who had a car and one other student to ride with him to be the recorder, and we paid them minimum wage, gave the driver a little bit for gasoline. It was a team of two students for each bus route. They would meet the bus at the starting point of that bus route one morning and record the distance from the driver's home to his first stop, who got on that bus, the school to which they were going, and the grades they were in. And then they would record the distance from the first stop to the second stop, and so on throughout the route.

When we got all this data and examined it, we found that some stops were so close together that the bus driver never got out of first gear. Then we decided which stops to eliminate. For example, if the first stop was a kindergarten student and at the second stop was a ninth-grader, we eliminated the second stop and made that ninth-grader walk to where the kindergarten student got on the bus. And we did that for every bus. We eliminated many, many stops, and in this way, we decreased the amount of gasoline that it took for a driver to make his run. Since we designated the location of the stops, if we found the driver was not following our plans, we called him in for a discussion. Each fall, the driver would make the same stops as the previous spring, except where new students got on the bus, until we completed the new survey. For three successive years, we made the survey, and that saved a lot of gasoline.

Then we started another policy. When the bus driver came in to gas up his bus one afternoon, we had the director of transportation follow that bus. The director of transportation had gasoline in a big can on his truck, which he used to fill up the bus at the end of the route as a way to determine how many gallons of gas the driver actually used on his route because he could measure how many gallons were left in the can. We suspected that many of the bus drivers were drawing gas out of their buses on weekends. To stop the siphoning of gasoline, we let them know up front that we were going to determine how much gas it took for them to make a run. At the end of the month, the driver had to make out a report, and if his gasoline use varied over 5 or 10 percent, we called him in.

Now we had some more accountability. As a way to prevent some defiance, I also recommended a pay increase for the bus drivers so they would have less reason to steal the gasoline.

So those were the two biggest areas of controllable expenses: school supplies and equipment and gasoline for the operation of the buses. We opened up for competitive bidding and established an accountability system, so if things had been falling through the cracks, we could minimize the crack falling. As we saved money, it was available to us to do some other things, and the conditions of the buildings sure needed the money.

CHAPTER 3
Buildings for Students

Another serious problem I faced was the dreadful deterioration of most of the school buildings in the county. Decades of "separate but equal" had resulted in dilapidated and outdated facilities. The overall condition of the physical plant was deplorable. Every child enters a physical plant for instruction, and it ought to be safe and reasonably adequate for the instructional program. So our first job was to assess the condition of each physical plant within each attendance area and establish priorities, since we didn't have enough funds to work on all of the problem areas at once.

In a school system the size of Macon County, which was in excess of 600 square miles, we had a variety of schools located in different parts of the county: west Macon, south Macon, east Macon, north Macon, and the Tuskegee area (the county seat and approximate geographical center of the county). So we also had to consider the communities in each area. In west Macon, known as the Shorter area, we had three schools: a K–3 school that fed into a 4–7 school that fed into an 8–12 school. The K–3 school was called Prairie Farms, and that was descriptive. The middle school was Shorter School, which fed into D. C. Wolfe High School. Shorter is about eighteen miles west of Tuskegee. In south Macon, we had a K–12 school called South Macon Elementary and High School, which was located about twelve miles south of Tuskegee. In the northern part of the county, we had an all-black school that was K–7, under segregation. That school fed into Tuskegee Institute High School, which was desegregated before I came to Macon County, as described in the introduction. There was also a K–12 school in the town of Notasulga, which was about nine miles north of Tuskegee. The elementary portion was the only all-white school when I went to Tuskegee in 1970. Notasulga High School, however, was integrated. There was also an elementary school, Nichols, located to the east of Tuskegee, whose students were bused to Tuskegee for high school. Within the city of Tuskegee were four elementary schools: Lewis Adams, Washington Public, Children's House (on the Tuskegee Institute campus), Tuskegee Public, as well as Tuskegee Institute High School.

We had to make a comprehensive study of all of the physical plants in the county—*comprehensive* because historically, when one section of the county learned that the board was spending some money in another section, they all descended on the board while saying, "Well, they got money down there to spend, so let's go get our share." When I realized how little had been done to maintain these buildings, I could understand their reasoning. So we had to be conscious of that and try to present the plan so that the folks would see that in the long run we could solve all the problems by establishing priorities. Generally, we had to make the case in such a way that the public would agree that whatever priority we set at number 1, they would agree that if they had that problem, they'd want that to be number 1 too. So when we established priorities, we had to have a series of meetings to explain to the publics—all the publics—why we placed this priority number 1, this priority number 2, and so forth. The idea was that we could solve each problem completely if we could spend all of the available money solving priority number 1 and then spending all the available money solving priority number 2, rather than patching up things here and there. We sold that idea. It was a hard work, but people saw our plan and supported it. And this procedure worked.

We determined that the situation in west Macon, where Prairie Farms, Shorter, and D. C. Wolfe schools were located, was the number 1 priority. Basically, there were two problems. First of all, the Prairie Farms School was literally falling down. Termites were eating it up. It was a frame building built in the late '30s, as I recall. I don't think we ever found any record showing it had been treated for termites. It was something to behold, a real dinosaur. The classroom was heated by potbellied stoves, and in one corner, you had a great big television set! What a sight—the past and the future there together. We went out one Saturday morning and crawled under the building. As a carpenter and former industrial arts instructor, I recognized immediately what was going on. The situation was even worse than I had nerve to convey to the public. I don't think that building would have stood up another two years. There was nothing to be done short of vacating it. And the public agreed with us.

A second problem in that area was that the D. C. Wolfe School, which had been built maybe in the late fifties, an all-brick building, had been built without a kitchen and cafeteria. They built a nice gymnasium-auditorium, but they didn't have enough money to build a kitchen and cafeteria. Now the Shorter School, which was only about one mile away, had a small cafeteria, but we couldn't serve D. C. Wolfe's whole student body in it at one time. So they bussed one-half of the high school student body to the Shorter School to eat each day. Therefore, students at that school ate a hot lunch every other day. As a first step, we consolidated all three schools into one administrative unit led by Mr. Guy Crawford, so we saved the money that had been paid for two additional principals. We then amassed enough money with state aid and local savings to build an addition to D. C. Wolfe School.

In regard to that addition, I made a recommendation which required a lot of explanation before the public bought it: that we add the K–3 classrooms to the high school so we could eliminate using the Prairie Farm School completely. Well, that went against the historical grain. Folks had been accustomed to adding the next lower grades to the high school. In this case, they were saying, "Let's move grades 5, 6, and 7 to the high school and send the K–3 students to Shorter School."

The addition to the Deborah Cannon Wolfe
High School on the day of dedication,
April 14, 1974.

When I inquired as to the purpose of that, they said, "Well, we don't want those high school kids to negatively influence the elementary kids." I said, "Well, number

29

1, they all ride on the same buses, and number 2, if that's the main worry, high school students are not going down there and trying to act big among K–3 students, and vice versa. You can tell the K–3 students, 'Don't go into that high school part,' and a larger percentage of those young students will obey that command than would seventh-grade girls trying to act big with the high school boys and vice versa. We don't have to worry about that influence, because nobody's trying to be big. In other words, if a high school student sees two third-graders fighting, he's going to try to break it up. But if a high school boy sees two seventh-graders, he may egg them on."

That idea was sold to the public, and they bought it.

We satisfied the parents in that attendance area, the D. C. Wolfe area, and incidentally prevented a potential disaster at the Prairie Farms School. We were able to come up with more than $250,000 to get that facility built at D. C. Wolfe. Prairie Farms School had about ten classrooms, so we built twelve new classrooms and situated the cafeteria in such a way that high school students could use it without going through the primary school, and the primary students could come in another entrance without going through the high school. And it worked out beautifully.

We carpeted all of the classroom floors and carpeted even the cafeteria. Again, I had to sell our board and other people on putting carpet in the cafeteria. Well, we got new carpet equipment, we trained our faculty and staff, and as far as I know, it worked out well. It decreased the noise factor and everything. So we were able to solve that problem.

The construction of the wing at D. C. Wolfe cost about $250,000, with $100,000 of the funds coming from the Impact Aid program.[1] With the construction at D. C. Wolfe, we satisfied the rest of the county that their turn was coming because they had agreed on the priorities.

The second order of priority was South Macon High School. Earlier we had been successful in obtaining federal funds to buy band instruments to start an instrumental music program at three of the high schools. Previously, only one high school had had a band; that was Tuskegee Institute High School (TIHS). So we were able to spend $30,000 of federal funds per high school to buy band instruments for South Macon and D. C. Wolfe. And we were able to find enough money to employ three full-time band directors out of local funds. But South

Macon did not have a gymnasium. They were still trying to play basketball games outside. They also didn't have facilities for band practice. They tried to practice in the cafeteria and the noise was disruptive through the whole building, because the cafeteria was located in the center of the building. So we eventually came up with enough money that we could start planning the addition to South Macon.

Here we encountered another problem: the school was built in swampland, and after they tested the soil, we found that the soil would not support the weight of the proposed gymnasium. So we had to do something extra by sinking pylons way into the ground and actually build on top of the pylons to keep it from sinking, which of course ran into greater costs. Nevertheless, we were able to provide a modern gymnasium with classrooms for physical education, a band room with individual practice rooms, storage, and two or three additional classrooms. That, as I recall, was about a $700,000 project, which solved the second-biggest problem in the district.

Now at the same time that we were undertaking these two major projects, we had to do emergency repairs all over the district, and we generally did that with our own maintenance crew. As I recall, we added one full-time maintenance person: a painter. When I recommended we hire a painter, I said, "We need to do this first. To meet our priorities, we've got to do what I call some 'cosmetic things.'" And when some people questioned my use of the term, I just said to them, "You know, the world would be in bad shape if we didn't have cosmetics. You think of all the uses of cosmetics. Some of these people you think are pretty, look pretty, because of cosmetics."

We had some frame buildings—one of them was at Shorter—that had never even been painted. We had some buildings over at Lewis Adams School that had never been painted, additions to the brick structure, that had never been painted. I said to the board, "You know if we had a painter, we could spend 400 or 500 dollars for paint. People need to see us doing something, and the best way to do it is to do something cosmetic on the outside rather than going on the inside of the building that's hidden from the public."

Of course, they understood my point, and it worked out beautifully. We had a little project going on at two or three schools, and we always painted the street side of the building first. And as folks passed by, they'd remark, "The school board sure is doing something, because there's paint going up."

Incidentally, and on a humorous note, when we advertised for a painter, a white female applied for the job. My maintenance men said, "We don't want to have no female." I said, "You know we can't discriminate." So we hired this lady. She was very shapely, and she wore a T-shirt that said, "Try it, you'll like it." She wore short britches too. But that woman climbed up on that ladder and folks passed by and saw her out there painting away. She did a good job too. She needed a job. She worked. When I asked, "Are you a painter?" she told me about things she'd painted and all that stuff and she had to have a job. You know, some people want a job until you hire them, but she wanted a job even after she got it. And she'd jump up on that ladder and sometimes she'd be out there by herself. I'd go by and see what she was painting, and the next day, she'd finished it. I mean, she did an excellent job.

Some things we had to do cosmetically so that our public would know that we were making efforts to improve all the schools. We had to do some of that stuff in every section, because while we had a number 1 and number 2 priority, there were some things in every unit that needed immediate attention. Those things were primarily what I call cosmetic, but they helped us out and kept a lot of folks from hollering about the money being spent in other areas of the county. For example, we had to do a lot of plumbing work. When a toilet would break down, they'd put up a sign that said, "Not working," but I said that the same people who put the sign up could go buy some screws and fix it. And then we replaced windowpanes that had been broken. These things made the school buildings more attractive and more comfortable for the students and teachers who were there.

In addition to these "cosmetic" and maintenance improvements, we installed a new roof on the high school portion of the Tuskegee Public building. We also installed completely new plumbing and fixtures, including toilets, new classroom doors and exit doors, and new tiling at Washington Public Elementary School. At Tuskegee Institute High School, the old building was completely renovated, including rewiring, new ceiling panels, new plumbing, new exit doors, outside lighting, and new tiling in many parts of the building. The auditorium received a new roof as well as new doors and fresh paint. Lewis Adams Elementary School received a new roof, rewiring and new fixtures, new exit doors, plumbing improvements, (e.g., a septic tank) and repainting. Since these schools were all located in the city of Tuskegee, these renovations were in part financed by the Model Cities program at a total cost of another $250,000.[2]

Early in my tenure, we contracted with the School of Education at Auburn University to conduct a study of the Macon County system and to make recommendations. Another study was undertaken by the Alabama Department of Education. And finally, we created a Blue Ribbon Panel of Citizens to conduct a similar study. All three entities made recommendations for improvements to physical plant and instruction. One of the major recommendations of all three groups was the construction of a comprehensive high school on land adjoining the current Tuskegee Institute High School.[3] Consequently, the board and I set into motion planning for a vocational technical school that would serve the entire county.

The facility that we planned would have offered courses to high school students in many career areas, including auto mechanics, upholstery, airplane mechanics, tailoring, plumbing and electrical wiring, paramedical specialties, and fine arts (e.g., drafting, ceramics, and theater). It was also envisioned that the facility could offer courses to the post-high school population in areas like woodworking, leather craft, and bookbinding. In addition to the technical areas, the school would offer a comprehensive program including a library/media center; language laboratory; home economics suites; science laboratories; business classrooms; rooms for photography and television production; rooms for voice, band, and orchestra rehearsals; an all-purpose gymnasium; a swimming pool; an auditorium with seating for 4,000 persons; a cafeteria; and a childhood development laboratory.

Outside the building, we proposed areas for a small lake, botanical garden, and small zoo. This multipurpose facility was on the drawing board and would have been constructed with a combination of local, state, and federal funds, had I remained in Macon County. In fact, we had already engaged a contractor and were in the initial phases of drawing up the contract when the 1976 elections changed the character of the school board and the plans were dropped. Unfortunately, this building was not constructed due to circumstances we'll discuss later.

A second consideration that influenced the physical plant and its utilization was not monetary or physical but psychological. At one time, Shorter School had an all-black high school and transferred the white students from Shorter into Tuskegee Public (Tuskegee High School). When D. C. Wolfe High School was built, Shorter became a middle school. In addition, there were white kids from east Macon who were bussed into Tuskegee Public, and the black kids from east Macon were bussed into Tuskegee Institute High School. So for a period of time, the city of Tuskegee had two high schools. Tuskegee High School (also known as Tuskegee Public) was located in the center of the city, just a block from the central office. Tuskegee Institute High School, a newer and larger facility, was located on the west side of town near Tuskegee Institute (now Tuskegee University). When the order came to desegregate the high schools, and whites found they could not prevent it, they started a movement to build a private academy. George Wallace helped to raise money for it because that was the first integrated school in the state of Alabama.

It's an intriguing story. The day they were supposed to carry out the integration of the school, George Wallace sent over 200 state troopers and militiamen, and they circled the school. There's a whole history of battles that went on, including the time he took over the schools, and he was hauled into federal court for his interference. So then they started raising money for the private academy and Macon Academy had already opened for business prior to my coming. (See introduction for further details.)

When I arrived there in 1970, the school board held the idea that if they kept Tuskegee High School open, the whites would eventually return there. It was my contention all along that if whites were going to return, we had to make the school of such superior quality that everybody who valued a good quality education would want to come to it. So long as we had inferior and dilapidated physical plants, had no challenging programs, and the schools were not accredited, we couldn't expect anybody to want to come to them. Still, the majority of the board members were of the opinion that they should keep Tuskegee Public open, because the whites might return. I said that while that may be praiseworthy on the one hand, our job was to try to make our schools as good as possible for the ones who were here and that worrying about the ones who were not here and trying to entice them to come back was a waste of time and energy, as well as money. We were spending an inordinate amount of time worrying about that problem. I pointed out that those who had gone probably had to save face among their friends and neighbors. When most of them left, they said that they would never return, and I maintained that when they can't afford the private school, they would move to another county to avoid returning here, as others had done. History has proven that my opinions were correct.

So the impact of desegregation and the loss of our white students to the private school had many ramifications which had to be faced. This situation raised a lot of questions for the people who had lived in Macon County all along. After a lot of research and soul searching, comparing the cost per pupil for water, electricity, and other costs, from one school to another—see chart on page 105—the trend was unmistakable: white student population in the county had dropped from 984 in 1961–1962 to 260 in 1970–1971. Those white students were primarily attending two schools: Tuskegee Public Elementary and Notasulga Elementary and High School. At Tuskegee High School, it was costing too much to educate the few students who attended there.

My family lived a block and a half from that school and some of my children attended Tuskegee High School. Melanie, my oldest, graduated from Tuskegee High, and both Eric and Laverne attended school there for a time. In addition to the small student population, maintenance over the years had been poor in part of the building. It was the oldest school building in Tuskegee. Along with Shorter School, which was probably the oldest in the county, and the Notasulga School, it was one of the three oldest buildings in Macon County. Then there was a fire at the school which destroyed the high school section. It had to be closed, and those students were transferred to Tuskegee Institute High School. We kept the rest of the building as an elementary school, and it's known as Tuskegee Public School.

This business of desegregation in Macon County created many tragedies. Let me tell you a story. One tragedy is what it did to some people, particularly very poor whites. There came a time when I was driving to the Notasulga School and I recognized what appeared to be a young girl who should have been in school. She was Caucasian. I stopped and talked with her and told her who I was. She was walking toward a filling station so I got out of the car and walked with her toward that. I asked her where she attended school. It turned out she was enrolled at Tuskegee Institute High School. And I asked her why she was not in school. She said, "The niggers up there don't like me." And I said, "Well, do you like them?" "Some of them I do." Then I said, "Well, who is being denied an education when you don't go to school?" "Well, I don't know. Most of my friends attend the private school." I found out where she lived and talked with her parents. They said, "We don't have money to send her to the private school." And I said, "You're not going to let her be educated?" "Well, she doesn't want an education. We'll just do without it." That girl never did come back to school as far as I know, although I made two or three follow-up visits. I even had a visiting teacher who called her. We couldn't do anything about saving her. I said, "Well, that's a tragedy that folks don't even know about. Here's this girl, fourteen or fifteen years old, the parents were uneducated, and they said they didn't have the money to send her to the Macon Academy. She was not a scholar, so she couldn't get a scholarship. Everyone wants to give scholarships to kids who are bright and who excel, but since she was not, she became part of the tragedy that folks just forgot about. And I said, "How many students are lost, just like this girl?" More than we could count.

The issue of integration of schools resulted in many problems. Macon County had a history of fires centered on the whole issue of segregation. The Shorter School at one time burned down. And Tuskegee High School burned, as just noted. On two occasions, someone tried to burn down Notasulga School, apparently to avoid desegregating the school. The year before I came there, some local whites tried to burn the Notasulga school down. They burned a significant portion of it down to the ground, but other whites along with the fire department were able to save part of the school.

Notasulga was the strongbed of the Ku Klux Klan in Macon County. Going back to the Scottsboro era in the early twentieth century, there was a black farmer in that northern section of the county who had bought a mule from a man and either he got behind on his payments or something, and they came with one deputy sheriff to confiscate the mule. About that period of time, the Communist Party was also active with farmers in the South and it tried to get black people to join that movement. The whites were upset about that. So when they came out to claim the mule, the man claimed that he didn't owe for it. He got a shotgun and shot at them and ran them away. Then the whites got a posse to round this man up (they were rounding up a whole lot of black folks then in the northern end of the county) with dreadful intentions. However, there was a white couple, businesspeople in town, who hid this black man under their kitchen table, so the posse didn't catch this man. They had come to lynch him, but the businessman was able to get the man out of the county. This couple had one son, who was a little kid then. When I came to Macon County, I met the Andersons, the couple who hid the man. They ran a five-and-dime store in Notasulga and had a history of being liberal, and liberal meant being nice to blacks and not joining efforts against them. They had also helped to save the burning school building.

The principal at Notasulga School when I arrived was a Protestant minister who had been out at Shorter School where they also had a big fire. His name was Rev. Harding, and he was a segregationist. When I first went to Notasulga, the student body was supposed to have been already integrated. I went to Notasulga to see a football game, and Rev. Harding was showing me around proudly. We went out to the field where they were playing football, and sure enough, the team was integrated. I said, "What's wrong with that? Look over there!" He had his chest all poked out. He didn't see what I was pointing at. I had to tell him. All the cheerleaders were white. I said, "What happened to the cheerleaders? Your football team looks like it's almost 50–50, but your cheerleaders are all white." Then he said, "Well, now, Mr. Superintendent, we got rules and regulations, and they have tryouts. Folk had to qualify." And he said a whole lot of other things about how the black girls didn't try out, or they didn't qualify. So I said, "Rev. Harding, Monday morning, I want you to walk down the halls and put your arm on the shoulder of some of these black girls and tell them they're qualified and you want them to come out for cheerleading." "Well, I don't think that's—" he started. "I'm not asking you to think about it. I'm telling you to do it. When's your next football game?" He told me. And I said, "When I come up here, I want to see the results of your good work."

When I went to the next football game, about 40 percent of the cheerleaders had "qualified," and they were out there hollering. For the rest of that first year, I had to fight with Mr. Rev. Harding; I had to fight him for everything I wanted him to do and almost had to give him directives to do each thing. Obviously, I had the rest of the county to supervise too, so I couldn't continue to do that. So I persuaded him it was in his best interest to retire.

With the position of principal open, I was looking around for a good replacement. Now the son of the Andersons, Robert Anderson, had finished Auburn University with his master's degree, but he was a single man. I talked to Robert about the guide to inclusive integration that GTEA had developed, and I went over that booklet and some other ideas and said, "There isn't anything sacred about one school, one queen." We went through this whole thing. He said, "Well, you've got good ideas about that." So I recommended Bob for the principalship. Later on, I learned about the Andersons being involved with the man being chased.

Actually, I had to do a selling job on that appointment. Number 1, he's a young man, number 2, he's single, but he was one of the best appointments we made. He went to work immediately. They started electing two of everything, one white and one black, and that procedure worked out well for that community. As of 2002, Notasulga has been the longest completely desegregated school in the county where the student body has remained 60–40 or 50–50. The whites are supportive of that school, and the blacks get along well. But Robert Anderson has been the key.

He's still there. Periodically, I hear from him. I went there recently and presented the commencement speech.

Three or four years ago, the board of education of Macon County wanted to consolidate all of the high schools, including Notasulga, at Tuskegee. Bob Anderson called me. They had a committee and had raised enough money to file a suit to keep the school board from including Notasulga in this consolidation effort. Bob asked me to come and testify in support of Notasulga's petition. After he talked with me, I said, "Well, Bob, the citizens of Notasulga supported us when we had a federal court order. So I will support you now."

The county was building a new high school, the Booker T. Washington High School, located just west of Tuskegee on Highway 80. It's a comprehensive high school, although not the vocational and technical school we had envisioned in the 1970s. (The architect, Major Holland, was the same man who had asked me some years back to design a program for a comprehensive high school; he used that plan in designing this building.) So the county wanted to bring Notasulga in and Notasulga went to court. The school board was disappointed because I testified as an expert witness in support of Notasulga remaining separate.

My contention was that historically, for the last twenty-five years, Notasulga, in compliance with the original court order, was the only integrated school in the county where both blacks and whites attended in almost equal numbers, and that when they played other schools that were all black, they gave all those other black schools an experience of interchanging in competitive athletics with an integrated school. So Notasulga not only supplied an integrated setting for its own students, when they went in athletic settings with other schools that were practically all black, it gave those students an experience across racial lines as well. I added that when everybody else was fighting to keep from desegregating the schools, the Notasulga community cooperated with the board of education in setting up what I think was the best example of an integrated school in the state of Alabama. Then I concluded, "Now when you destroy the Notasulga school, you're going to bring those white students, assuming all of them come. They're going to be a hundred students among 1,500 black students. With this ratio of black to white, you're still not going to have one desegregated school in the whole county. Since Notasulga cooperated with the board in desegregating their local school, it would be a slap in the face to take this integrated school away from them and deny the entire county the experience of an integrated school."

The court agreed with us.

The opposition questioned when I first went to Tuskegee and whether or not I was an expert witness. The judge said, "Now here's a man who served as superintendent here; he was here to desegregate the faculty through all of this; he has been superintendent of schools in New York. What more qualification do you have to have to be an expert witness?" When the judge ruled, he quoted a lot of my testimony. The board appealed the decision, but the appellate court upheld the original decision. I was pleased with that, but some folks got angry with me because I did it. I still think that was the right thing to do.

CHAPTER 4
Student Achievement and Curriculum Changes

Having noted the decrepit physical plant and the serious financial disarray that afflicted the Macon County Schools when I arrived, I could hardly have expected superior academic performance from the students who were victims of such a poor academic environment. So I was not surprised to learn that a majority of our students were reading two or more grades below grade level. In fact, our statistics showed that the longer a student remained in the Macon County Schools, the farther behind he or she was likely to fall.[1]

Clearly, this condition needed to be addressed. However, first we had to acknowledge the negative attitudes many in the public and within the educational community held, which blamed the students and/or the parents for these failures. Here is an excerpt from some plans and projections I made early in my tenure to a group of educators:

> Let me close with a statement about factors influencing the wholesome pupil growth and achievement, which are resident in the pupil himself.
>
> I know, to my own satisfaction, that in order for one to learn, he must take an offensive attitude. Many of our students are extremely defensive, and all too often those of us in education have been guilty of helping to solidify him in this extreme defensive position, in spite of our honest quest to help him overcome.

We must help him to know that he is not really *educationally depressed* but *educationally cheated.*

We must help him to know that he is not socially deprived but *socially ostracized.*

We must help him to know that he is not economically disadvantaged but economically swindled.

We must do and say the kind of things which will make poor whites and blacks go on the mental and intellectual offensive. We must stop using the conscience-soothing terminology invented by those who are the cause of the asinine, oppressive, and degrading procedures and practices.

For when you tell someone that he's been swindled, cheated, ostracized, he's a little set back at first, and then he recovers.

First, he wants to know what and who. He takes the offensive. Students who are behind or different in their achievement must know that they are behind. They must know why they are behind. We must reject the psychology which says, "Let's make believe that something else is the condition," for while we are making believe, the students are getting further and further behind.

But they also must know that it is within their power to not only catch up, but to be in the lead.

Wholesome pupil growth and achievement are affected by factors resident in materials of instruction, the curriculum, the teaching-learning situation, the socio-physical environment, and the pupil himself. I have discussed the physical environment in a previous chapter and my beliefs about the pupil in the preceding paragraphs. The remainder of this chapter will address the curriculum and the teaching-learning situation and our efforts to improve both factors during my tenure at Macon County Schools.

All of our instructional program improvement came through funded programs since our local budget was already taxed to meet the needs of teachers for instructional supplies, transportation, and physical plant improvements. We received assistance from the local Model Cities program and applied for many grants through the federal government. Based on our student need, we were eligible for some of the basic programs like Head Start and Follow Through that were nationwide programs. Other reading programs included the Cureton Reading Program in the fifth and sixth grades and the Compensatory Reading and Arithmetic Project (CRA). Reading was a primary focus of our curriculum efforts.

Still other programs required us to do serious scrutiny and research as well as utilize grant-writing expertise to gain funding for the projects I visualized. One of the most unique programs was funded under the Title VIII Dropout Prevention Program. Others were the Parenting Program and the Piano/Reading program. Each of these was very special. We also received funding for an ongoing teacher in-service program. I'd like to consider each of these in more detail.

A dear friend and colleague who first worked with me in Gainesville, Georgia, Jerry Hollingsworth, did the research that led to our Dropout Prevention program. We had to prove that we had a dropout problem and Jerry did the statistics for us. You see, many of our dropouts were invisible. They left the system and were not recorded in the official dropout rate for many reasons. Jerry went back through the permanent records and tracked the number of students each year in school, and it became clear that the number of dropouts was serious.

According to the grant proposal, Macon County, along with many school systems throughout the United States, kept dropout records only on those students who informed the school of their intent. The students who simply failed to return to school at the beginning of an academic year or following an extended vacation were simply dropped from the rolls and so they usually failed to appear on the official school records as dropouts. On the basis of these records, the rate of dropouts for the previous four years was 7.58 percent. Because we were aware that this number only reflected the announced dropouts, we conducted a comprehensive study of the population of the target school (Tuskegee Institute High School) for the past four years and found that the actual percentage of dropouts was 9.4 percent. This data was collected by systematic analysis of individual enrollees whose names were deleted from school records prior to the time that enrollees received a diploma from the school system.

In order to locate these "summer dropouts," a study was undertaken in which all seventh-grade first-month enrollees for a given year (1964–1969) were traced by name until their present status was confirmed. Where records proved inadequate, the researchers contacted parents, teachers, principals, neighbors, and peers of the students to confirm his/her status. This study revealed that more students drop out during the summer (i.e., fail to return to school the following year) than drop out during the year.

Thus, tracing students by name, we determined that from May of 1969 to September of 1969, nearly *one and one-half times as many students dropped out in the summer as in the preceding school year.*[2]

Having thus established the seriousness of the dropout problem in Macon County, the next step was to devise and implement a program to stem the tide. The ideas that became the Title VIII Project ARISE came out of my own experience. For example, people assumed that the absence of certain parents in school activities demonstrated a lack of interest. At one time, I agreed with that assumption. Then I realized that is a fallacy. Some people are so busy trying to acquire the basic necessities that many of us take for granted that they don't have time to come and "fool around" with school. I know that my mother would come to school when we got into some difficulty or trouble. However, she only had one dress, so if that dress was dirty, she wouldn't come to school *except* if one us was in serious trouble. So based on that memory, I realized that if we wanted to prove to parents that being involved with their child's education was important, we needed to make it worth their while to learn and exhibit behaviors that other parents who came to school regularly exhibited. So we decided to use minimum wage to motivate a group of these parents. I had to argue with the folks in Washington about this wage business. I told them, "I don't want to pay a poverty wage. These folks are already in poverty! How you going to get them out of poverty paying a poverty wage?"

First, we identified students who were at risk of dropping out of school. The criteria for identifying these students were the following:

1. excessive absenteeism and tardiness,
2. retentions resulting in the student being two or more years behind his/her grade,
3. underachievement based on teacher comments and predictions, and
4. failure in English for two or more semesters and/or failure of four required subjects.

About 350 students were thus identified.

Then we selected a group of parents (about thirty) who had the largest number of students on the at-risk list in their household and offered them jobs as a parent-counselor aides (PCA) to act as paraprofessional attendance officers and counselors. Their job description was to exhibit behaviors that we knew to be supportive of student success and to monitor the attendance, grades, and discipline problems of not only their own children but also a caseload of ten to twelve other students from their neighborhood. For this work, we paid the PCAs $100 a week and provided support and training. The average parent we employed had only six years of school, so we also required them to enroll in adult basic education. We thought that not only would this enable them to help their children with homework, but it would set an example about the importance of education. The parents could tell their children that they too had to deal with problems of attending classes and doing homework!

There is one thing about extremely poor people: they have a rapport with one another that middle-class folks don't have. They'll walk in the house and say, "Honey, I want to take a bath. My bathtub's not working." Or they might need to come over to see if Marilyn has some clothes to wear to school tomorrow. And if necessary, the PCA will help her wash her dress and iron it. She'll do that because the next morning that parent's going to be up at the high school to check attendance, and if anybody on her list is not present, it's her job to get out and find him and bring him on to school. If the principal is getting ready to suspend one of her students, she's going to argue with the principal on behalf of the student. So that was the main part of the program.[3]

In addition, we were able to fund two high school counselors whose main focus was to work with these at-risk students through individual and group counseling. A teacher and seven teacher aides also supplemented the English staff at the high school. We also instituted a work-study program in brick masonry and auto mechanics for the target school, with preference given to our Title VIII students. A parent-counselor aid coordinator monitored, trained, and supervised the PCAs, along with a director and other office staff.

This program was initially funded at $150,000, and funding was increased the following year to $350,000; it continued for two additional years. As a result of the program, the dropout rate declined by 99.3 percent and absenteeism declined by 66 percent in the first year at the target school.[4]

Evaluation reports submitted to the US Office of Education indicate that the improvements in attendance and lowering of dropouts continued throughout the life of the project. It was also found that many residual effects of the program were evident even after the program ended. Parents who had been employed by the program continued their watchful support of their own and neighboring children, but at a reduced level consistent with their need to find employment elsewhere, leaving them with less time to visit their neighbors and the school. In fact, former PCAs discontinued attendance at PTA meetings and adult education by 70 percent to 80 percent. Nevertheless, student behaviors showed continued improvement as absences remained less than 50 percent of the pre-project rate, suspensions increased but did not surpass the baseline numbers, but the dropout rate was higher than expected. These data point out the need for continuous support and interactions of family with the school to prevent dropouts. Although the study only followed the subjects for one year after the project ended, some residual effects seem likely, while the impact of having a parent directly involved in school supportive behavior is also apparent.[5]

Some of the professional people were concerned that these folks were buying old raggedy cars and others were buying television sets, etc. The critics said we should give them a class to teach them how to use their money! I refused to do that. After all, what do most people do when they get their first job? Buy a car, of course. It was logical to do what they were doing.

Some of the PCAs went on and got their GED diplomas, but the main thing was the children saw their parent reading books and studying, so they could relate to the work the student was doing. And the example carried over to the younger siblings in the family too. I am convinced this program made an impact on these younger children even though we weren't able to conduct a follow-up for long enough to provide the proof.

We also required PCAs to attend the PTA meetings and to bring two or three other parents with them. So here are parents visiting the school, meeting the teachers and principals, and getting used to how things are done there. All of these behaviors make a difference in middle-class families, and we now had poor families emulating these behaviors *as their job*.

I had to argue with two Washington bureaucrats that we had a viable program. They were talking about funding the Tuscaloosa program instead of ours. They said this program wouldn't work, and I replied, "How do you know? You never tried it!" But with this program in place, students had an advocate, someone admonishing them to get up on time and get to school, cooking breakfast, all to keep getting that paycheck. When the program ended, they were sick. Some of them had gotten off welfare and made big improvements in their lives. Unfortunately, Macon County did not have the funds to carry on this program when the federal funding ended in 1975.

Another program that addressed the problem of dropouts was the Preparation for Parenthood Program. Many of our female students dropped out of school due to pregnancy or the need to care for an infant. We asked, "What is the most important problem facing the female student with a baby that keeps her from returning to school?" Obviously, the answer was, "Who's gonna keep my baby?" So we developed a program for a grant that turned out to be research oriented. We got $55,000 funding from the Model Cities program for construction of the building which supplemented the $139,000 from the Department of Health, Education, and Welfare.[6]

Part of my idea was forged by a picture I saw in *Time* magazine about a school in California that was encouraging girls to come back to school. Here was a girl sitting in a trigonometry class with a baby on the desk and milk bottles. I asked myself, "How in the world can she concentrate on trigonometry with a crying baby in front of her? You haven't made any adjustments to meet the unique needs of this student." So we developed a different kind of program that *would* meet the needs of the mother and the child.

> The two components, Preparation for Parenthood and Early Childhood Development make up the one program and each component will be in support of the other but will maintain a certain degree of independence.
>
> Specific objectives of the Child Development Program include: educational materials equal with the age and development of children up to thirty months, proper nutrition and medical services, and providing a day care center to enable the child's mother to complete school."[7]

The program required that we have professional care for the babies, including an isolation unit for a sick child. We also had classes for the mothers and mothers-to-be for which they got high school credit while learning to better care for their children. We provided transportation for the girls and their babies, on the school bus in many cases, food, clothing, a nursery for the babies, a nurse, and counselor, as well as several paraprofessionals. So the girls could see we weren't playing. The girls came out of the woodwork when they saw that we had a program designed for them.

Oh, the good Christian folks got mad at me for what they saw as encouraging girls to have babies out of wedlock. (One thing that helped was that I had two daughters at the school myself.) Actually, the program did just the opposite. When the other students saw how hard the mothers had to work to finish their education while taking care of their children, the pregnancy rate went down significantly at the high school. And every year it got lower.

One time I almost fired the director because I heard her talking to the girls about the mistakes they had made. I said to her in private, "Girls have been having babies since the beginning of time. Don't talk about babies being a mistake. Just because they had a baby before finishing high school is not the most serious mistake of their lives." So we got rid of that sort of talk. Our approach was positive: where do you go from here and how can we help you? One girl, who at nineteen had three babies, managed to not only complete high school, she also went on to college.

The program was only in place for five years, but I'm sure it made a great contribution. Unfortunately, when I left Macon County, the program was dismantled completely.[8]

Another area of concern was the deplorable reading test scores. Throughout my tenure, the system developed and supported many programs to address this need, many of which were nationally known through federal funding, such as Head Start, Follow Through, and Title I. We tried out every program that we thought would help our students, and each of these had a reading component. In addition, we created a system-wide program for fourth grade students, which used an experimental program called the Cureton Reading Program. But by far, the most interesting and innovative program of all was the piano reading program that was part of Project Read.

The way I see it is that you can't get money out of the bank unless you put money in it. By the same token, you have to put understanding of words, letters, pronunciation, and meaning of words into the student's head to get reading out. If they learn to read early enough, they have fewer problems with all of their subjects.

With that in mind, I thought about piano playing. I asked myself and others, "Can you think of anybody in elementary school who could play piano and could not read or acted like a dodo in class?" Nobody could think of a single one. I did informal surveys, and everybody came up with the same answer. So then I wondered, *Did the piano playing have anything to do with the fact that these kids were academically successful?* So I continued to brainstorm with a couple of my staff members in the research and development department. We reasoned that if students could learn sharps and flats, quarter notes and half notes and the like on the piano and on sheet music, they should be able to transfer these same skills to mathematics and reading. If they can develop the visual acuity to follow the notes on the line and staff where they jump all over, they should be able to read on a straight line.

As we stated in the grant proposal,

> One need not cite the overwhelming evidence that economically poor students and ethnically different youngsters often come to the public schools with insufficient pre-reading readiness skills. The project developers believe that systematic instruction in basic piano lessons oriented toward reading skills can significantly improve the critical listening and pre-reading readiness level of students. Consequently, the program involves teaching music. Because of children's natural high interest and innate love of music in general, it is an excellent tool which can be used to motivate children to achieve in other areas of academic and aesthetic learning.[9]

Thus, our research department, in conjunction with Tuskegee Institute's department of music, developed a program where we would teach piano to elementary students. At first, we couldn't get it funded, so we changed the focus to teaching reading through the piano, and we got funding to equip a bus with electronic pianos, including a console where the teacher could listen to each student individually. Then we hired an excellent reading teacher, who also taught piano and music, to teach primary students the basics of piano playing. To fuse the two subjects together, the teacher would stress the letters of the alphabet that name the notes on the staff. She also taught basic mathematics in teaching about the notation of quarter, half, and whole notes. In addition, she pointed out the similarity between reading music and words by following a line from left to right and from top of the page to the bottom.

We had an assistant who drove the bus and shepherded the students in groups of six or eight to the bus. They went to a different elementary school each day of the week and taught those kids. This program generated a lot of excitement. Not only were the kids excited and ready when the piano bus arrived at their school, but the parents were pleased that their little Johnny or Susie was learning to play the piano. People who couldn't afford private lessons encouraged their children, especially their little girls, to do well in the class, and that spilled over to other subjects too.

Unfortunately, we weren't able to prove the impact of the piano program on reading scores, but the motivational factor alone made it worthwhile, and we did see overall improvement in reading and mathematics in the system. In fact, I was so heartened by the response to this idea that when I went to New York, we were able to install an electronic piano classroom with local funds. Some people from the Roosevelt School System have told me how this piano lab got them started learning music and they now play piano in their churches.[10]

Another new program, the Cureton Reading Program, was implemented in December 1971 in grades 5 and 6 through the Emergency School Assistance Program. The program was implemented throughout the county and included students who were also a part of the CRA program (students who were two or more grades below level in reading). The Cureton program consisted of packets of prepackaged materials which were used in classrooms for lessons in decoding and comprehension skills. After only three and a half months, positive results were reported in test scores.[11]

Likewise, the Fourth Grade Reading Program was implemented in 1971–1972 under the auspices of Model Cities and the Macon County Board of Education's Educational Development Center. After intensive assessment of needs and attitudes of the educational staff and community, the project staff created a model with basic and supplementary reading materials, curriculum guide, and bimonthly in-service meetings.

New materials placed in each fourth grade class were Houghton Mifflin textbooks and workbooks on six different reading levels; audio-visual phonics records and charts; high interest, low-level storybooks; duplicator masters for enrichment exercises; and reading skill builder kits.

The curriculum guide was developed cooperatively by the fourth grade teachers and reading staff. The guide was constructed as a practical aid to satisfy student and teacher needs. It helped the teacher to give guidance not only to the pupil on and above grade level but to the pupil below grade level as well. The guide was also intended to help teachers develop their own techniques to fit their particular situation.

The bimonthly in-service meetings were held for the purpose of discussing and demonstrating methodological techniques for teaching reading skills. These meetings aided the teachers in the use of the materials provided for each fourth grade class.[12]

After just four months, the staff found improvements in both listening and reading performance by the pupils. Just as important, the comments from the teachers were both positive and enthusiastic, generally asking that the program be continued.

It is my contention that four basic principles are mandatory to design and install curricular changes that meet the *felt need* of the difficult student (many of whom are minority students).

1. We must speedily bury the assumption of many educators that the same medicine which worked in our schools for the "others" is good enough for these. We have merely manipulated the dosage by diluting or strengthening the concentration. I say that for these difficult students, just providing the same kind of medicine is not enough. New models must replace the old where the need is clear. We must have a new kind of medicine.

2. We must purge from our thought pattern the notion that different cultures (or subcultures) are of necessity competitive alternatives. We must see them as intertwined in the wholeness of American culture. In other words, reject the deficit and different models and replace them with the concept of biculturation.

3. We must all know and understand thoroughly what many researchers are saying about the effects on pupils (I add especially many difficult and/or

minority pupils) of a teacher's values, beliefs, attitudes, and expectations. It is imperative that we teachers and administrators learn how to raise our own level of expectation of pupil performance, especially of minority students.

4. We must understand that the literature is replete with various models which may be suggestive in bringing about curriculum change. In my opinion, none are inclusive of a structural framework through which a new kind of marriage "in the dynamics of a school-based continuing research effort aimed at significant and positive changes helpful to minority students may be realized."[13]

From the foregoing ideas, Macon County Schools adopted an in-service program to upgrade and reshape the skills and attitudes of its teaching and administrative staff. This program of staff development was both novel and intuitive at the time and has been replicated in many places in later years. We developed a series of mini-courses and the board of education required each certified staff member to take at least two mini-courses during the first year of operation. Student achievement gains were the constant focus for all courses, but each was designed to meet the needs of different personnel. Many were taught by local staff members, but outsiders with special skills were brought in when we did not have people on staff who could address the needs expressed by our employees.

The courses were all designed to stimulate our staff to modify, evaluate, and adapt their current methods of teaching and supervising to help our pupils develop to their full potential. Mini-courses were designed to deal with such diverse topics as metric mathematics, career education, drug education, performance objectives, individualized instruction, questioning skills, and listening skills. In addition, special courses were created to meet the needs of such groups as principals, school counselors, and other support staff. Some of the mini-courses related to specific subject areas, such as history, mathematics, and music instruction, while others were more generic and reached across subject area divisions. I think this emphasis on staff development sent an unstated message to students and the community that education does not stop even when a person has a college degree and a good job, but continues. It also spoke to our desire to continue to find ways to be better at our jobs, and this is a positive message to send.

CHAPTER 5
I Riled Wallace

When I came to Macon County, I had already established a network of people who were of inestimable value to our work, and many also became personal friends. While the principal in Gainesville, Georgia, I was selected to serve on the Southeastern Education Laboratory due to my presidency of the all-black high school principals association in Georgia. In fact, some of the members were instrumental in putting my name forward for the position of superintendent of Macon County Schools, including Dr. Truman Pierce, dean of the School of Education at Auburn University, and Dean Hunter at the School of Education at Tuskegee Institute (now Tuskegee University).

Within a short time, I realized that the people at the State Department of Education in Montgomery were also open to helping us. Working with the Tuskegee Model Cities programs and our own research and development department, we began submitting proposals for many federal grants. Many of these were funded, so I gradually built a base of support among the people who supervised these grants. In short, everyone I had contact with in the educational infrastructure seemed ready to lend a hand, whether local, state, or federal. Even Governor George Wallace had been ready to acknowledge and support the school system. I say this not to brag but to lay the groundwork for what was to come later.

I had also been a founding member of the National Association of Black School Superintendents (NABSS), which later became the National Association of Black School Employees (NABSE). Through this organization, I developed contacts across the country with other highly placed black school leaders.

In 1972, just two years after my arrival in Macon County, the Alabama Educational Television Commission (AETC), which operated eight stations, was due for a renewal of license hearing before the Federal Communications Commission. Some months before this hearing, I received a telephone call from an unknown male who stated that he was the attorney for a group of plaintiffs who were prepared to oppose this license renewal. He said that they had an airtight case, but that they wanted somebody to testify who could qualify as an expert witness. He added that since I was a county superintendent involved with carrying out a federal court order to desegregate its faculty, he was sure he could have me declared an expert witness. I replied to him that although I was hired by the board of education in Macon County, I was paid through state funds, making me an employee of the state of Alabama, and he was asking me to testify against another arm of the state of Alabama—technically against my employer. I said to him, "That's a tall order! I have not met you, and I cannot give you an answer at this time." He replied that he could understand my position, but he needed somebody to testify that the state programming on these public stations did not consider nor include the needs of black citizens and also somebody to testify about the AETC's employment record. Then he asked me how much time I would need to make my decision about testifying, and I asked for a couple of weeks. He promised to get back to me then.

It was the most agonizing decision I have ever made. The issue that went rapidly through my head was that I had one child in college and three more coming along that I would need to provide for. So one factor I had to consider was personal financial responsibilities. I also wondered what would happen to all of our educational programs and plans that needed state support if I lost the good graces of state officials. I had trouble enough as it was, trying to run the school system with deficits and everything. But we depended primarily upon the state of Alabama for fiscal support, and even the federal program funds were funneled through the state. So a second factor was the financial health of the school system that I was charged with supervising.

I thought about Governor George Wallace and how vicious he could be when politically challenged, as I was being asked to do, and I knew that some of my supporters would simply fade away. Also, I didn't know what kind of personal danger I might be exposing myself and my family to. That was a third factor I had to consider.

THE ALABAMA EDUCATIONAL TELEVISION NETWORK

. . . Approaching

"Total Communications Service" For All Alabamians

An AETV pamphlet made it clear that the network served white students. There were many photographs in the pamphlet, and all of them pictured white people.

I did not have anyone at the local level that I felt I could discuss this decision with and maintain strict confidentiality. Nor was anyone else in my unique position with the peculiar weight on their shoulders that I had. So I called several superintendents among my acquaintances who I thought would understand the difficulties of my position. Here is where my NABSS brethren were indispensable. I had to make sure they were people who could understand the magnitude of the decision and who I could be certain would not betray my confidence. Many of these people asked the same questions that had already gone through my mind.

All my life, I have heard voices speaking to me. My wife says I should stop saying that, but it's true. Ideas just seem to pop into my mind. If I tarry and seek divine guidance, something comes into my mind! It came to me one night completely out of context. I was not able to sleep and I got up that night and this voice just said to me, "Do the right thing." I was not conscious that I was thinking about this decision at the time, but it was the only thing I had been agonizing over. It became clear to me that night that the state of Alabama, along with the Alabama Educational Television network, had always discriminated against blacks, so how could I live with myself as a member of the class being discriminated against to not take this opportunity to testify as an expert witness? I thought, *Why am I hesitating? I can get another job!*

That's how I decided to testify at the hearing on behalf of the plaintiffs. I testified that because of the system of discrimination against blacks in the education program, we were forced to do some things to try to bridge the gap between education denial and what the kids needed and that it worked an extreme hardship on us. (On p. 121, see letter from which statement was read.) There was another person, although I didn't know it at the time, who also decided to testify. She was also a former principal in Georgia, now serving as a full professor in the School of Education at Tuskegee: Dr. Frankie Ellis.

The FCC used two to three sentences from my statement and about the same from Dr. Frankie Ellis's statement, and based on these statements, it denied the license renewal to the state of Alabama.

> Dr. Frankie Ellis, a black woman who has chaired the Department of Teaching Disciplines at Tuskegee Institute since 1966, testified that she knew of no black teacher who had been invited to appear as an instructor on the AETC network, and that no black members of the faculty at Tuskegee Institute have been solicited by the SDE to help prepare curricula for in-school instructional programming. This evidence was uncontradicted by the AETC.[1]

Dr. Ellis testified that innumerable studies have pointed up broad discrepancies between Alabama's black and white communities in education achievement due in part to histories of racial segregation and economic deprivation. She emphasized that in order effectively to serve the needs of black students in Alabama, educational television must offer programming aimed at compensating for the educational lag of black students. Particularly, she noted that black children have special needs for black characters and teachers to emulate and identify with in order to help them develop positive attitudes toward learning and toward themselves. Likewise, Dr. Edgar Epps, a professor of urban education at the University of Chicago, testified that black Alabamians have developed cultural patterns and have educational needs that differ substantially from those of whites ...

For example, while 15.7% of Alabama's white population were below the poverty line in 1969, 52.9% of the black population were below that level ...

The preponderance of the evidence adduced by petitioners establishes that special needs which could not be served by AETC's avowed programming policy which considered race to be an irrelevant factor in designing its offerings. To this end, Mr. Ulysses Byas, the Superintendent of the Macon County Alabama Board of Education, testified that it was his experience that the majority of black students in Alabama enter school less well-prepared than white students to perform successfully in the classroom and that, in order to be effective, an educational system must act to deal with different levels of preparation. Petitioners have thus convincingly shown the need of Alabama's black population for effective educational programming through—compensatory programming, programming to which blacks can relate and programming relating to black history and culture, and have demonstrated that integrated programming can be but one factor in meeting these needs.[2]

The foregoing quotes were published by the FCC in their ruling that denied the renewal of licensure to the state of Alabama but allowed the state to reapply for the license in competition with any other groups that were interested. The ruling was dated February 8, 1972.

In a letter dated January 13, 1975, State Superintendent of Education LeRoy Brown stated,

> I am taking this opportunity to make it clear that the FCC's decision included the provision that the Educational Television Commission may apply for a new license and may continue telecasting until a new license is authorized. It is our understanding that the AETC will reapply for a license to operate the State ETV Network. In the interim, in-school programming will continue throughout the remainder of this school year of 1975-76, and thereafter. Your State Department of Education is concerned for the future of educational television in Alabama. We will make every effort to ensure that the quality and content of programming to our citizens, with special emphasis on the service provided to schools, will continue ...

It is clear to me that considerable negotiating had occurred between the state of Alabama and the FCC. In fact, the commission report ordered further hearings investigating the matters raised in the 1972 hearing. I wrote a letter to Mr. Lewis Paper in Washington, DC, following up on my statement at the hearing in November 1972. In that letter, I discussed my observations about the differences in the educational and economic status of blacks and whites and how those differences impacted on the school system.

What matters is that state officials, from Governor Wallace on down, were aware of my testimony in opposition to the license renewal very soon after the hearing. What matters even more is that the repercussions of my testimony were very quick in coming. In fact, I started having difficulty with various state officials almost immediately. State agencies that had been very cooperative became very distant. Telephone calls would not be returned. And from that time on, a lot of things happened. Foremost among them was the quest to find some area where I was not following the laws of the state so that officials could justify removing me from office.

Excessive auditing of our books was the most blatant example. In Alabama, there are two departments that do auditing of public books: the Department of Public Accounts, which usually audited school districts, and the state examiners, which usually audited city and county governments. These latter were referred to as political auditors. Well, after my testimony at the FCC hearing, the state sent the state examiners to Macon County. These people came to my office flashing their badges and said they were here to audit our books. Since we had already been audited by the Department of Public Accounts and I had had no experience with this agency, I told them I would have to talk to my attorney before letting them see our books. They told me they would be back in three days.

Our attorney, Tom Bradney, had his office in Alexander City. I called him and explained what had occurred. He replied that he had not known of the state examiners ever auditing school books, but he said they could legally do so. However, he added, "Don't let them take the books out of your office." When they returned, the first thing they asked was to take our books to Montgomery. I insisted that on my attorney's advice, I would not let them take the books anywhere, but I would give them space to do their work in my office. Finally, they agreed to my terms and we set them up in a conference room near my office.

They were at my office so long that they began to receive their paychecks there. Sometimes, they were so loud and using inappropriate language that I had to admonish them about it and threaten to throw them out if they continued to disturb and disrupt the work and the decorum of the superintendent's office. Eventually, they brought in a portable photocopier. They would make copies of purchase orders and then they would contact the company to verify the date, items, and amount of the purchase. Then they would randomly select canceled checks and do the same thing. They spent over a year in that room going through everything with a fine-tooth comb.

Apparently, somebody told them that I had sold a tractor. Prior to my arrival in Tuskegee, a previous superintendent had purchased a tractor with Title I funds. After I took over, the city of Tuskegee was discussing the need for a tractor and its plans to purchase one. Since ours was almost unused, and since the city had supported some of our programs through the Model Cities Program, I suggested to the board of education that we loan our tractor to save the city more than $30,000. The board agreed, and we lent the tractor to the city with the understanding that if we had a need for the tractor, the city operator would come and do the job. All of this was recorded in the board's minutes. The auditors couldn't find this reference and wanted me to locate it for them, but I refused. I told them it was there and it was their job to find, not mine. I had plenty of other work to do running the school district. Evidently, they did find the authorization, and that ended that accusation.

I always made sure decisions were recorded in the minutes and that the board was fully apprised of and supported every decision. You see, when I came to Tuskegee, there were people who said I should do things the way the past superintendents had done them. I replied that I didn't want to know anything about past practices. Instead, I wanted to know what the book said. If past practice didn't conform to the book, I wanted to change the practice. And that was a sound decision, because I didn't have the authority as superintendent of schools to let any other agency use school property without board approval. So it was in the minutes that the board had authorized the lending of that tractor.

After many months, the state examiners reluctantly told me the books were in good shape and they would be leaving soon. And they left.

But the next Monday morning, the chief auditor, who had told me the books were fine, was transferred, and another person was put in charge of the auditing team. They came back and stayed another three or four months.

Finally, they decided that we had done something wrong and they brought up charges against the superintendent and the board of education. What they charged us with went back to the year I was hired. At that time, the state law specified a certain salary for the superintendent of Macon County Schools. The board members said that the law was up for a change to increase that salary. The law also stated that a person hired as superintendent could not receive a raise during the time of his contract. So the board hired me with a clause in the contract stating that when the law raised the ceiling on the salary (it was a difference of about $1,800 per year), it would pay me that amount retroactively. We understood from the public auditors that this practice was common all over the state of Alabama. Nevertheless, these state examiners brought charges against us. First, they demanded that I repay the money, and I refused. Then they demanded the money from the board members, and they refused.

Our refusal set in motion the procedure of a hearing on the charges in Montgomery. The chief auditor and four or five other auditors comprised the hearing authority. They said that the hearing would take place in the morning and the ruling would be announced that afternoon. So we went to Montgomery, presented our case, and went to lunch, expecting the ruling to be ready that afternoon. Instead, the chief auditor said that they were unable to make a decision that day and it would be ready in a couple of days.

Two days later, there was still no decision. We had received the definite impression that the chief auditor was in our corner on this matter. After several more days of indecision, this chief auditor asked the state attorney general to rule on our case. The state attorney general was elected statewide, independently of the governor, and he was not in the Wallace camp. The attorney general ruled in our favor. Within a week, there came news that the chief auditor had committed suicide by blowing his brains out. I am convinced that the pressure Wallace and his supporters put on the chief auditor was so great that he chose to end his life. Wallace was unable to get rid of me through legal means. This man, the chief auditor, had been a World War II veteran and was an honest man.

Prior to my tenure in Macon County, there were a lot of questionable activities involving money, but I put a stop to them when I set up my system of accountability. I had a purchasing agent who said I should use a rubber stamp as the previous superintendent did, but I said no. I wanted every purchase order on my desk, and I would read and sign every one of them myself. The law stating that the board of education had to authorize every purchase over $1,500 had been ignored, but again, I made sure all those purchases were brought before the board and approved. I was suspicious that materials were being diverted to the private school by members of my staff.

My secretary had been in the habit of opening the mail for the previous superintendent, but I insisted that all mail addressed to the superintendent or the board be placed on my desk unopened. Then I would have the secretary sit in my office while I opened the mail and dictated my replies.

On occasion, I would go to the post office and pick up the mail myself. By doing this, I stopped whatever might have been going on with orders for materials going to places they didn't belong. That upset a lot of people, but it protected me and the public funds that taxpayers expected to be used in the public schools. After all, many of my staff had students enrolled in the private school and they may have thought they could take things from us to use there. Likewise, the gasoline accountability system that I had set in place upset enough people to create the crisis of having no gasoline delivered. Before we put in the huge tanks and took control of the delivery of gasoline, I would have on my desk a big stack of delivery slips that were signed by people I couldn't identify. I never wanted to make public allegations of theft because it would have been difficult to prove, but I solved the problem by changing the way the gasoline was delivered and put it under our control. I'm certain in my mind's eye that Wallace and his supporters were behind the siphoning off of public funds to the "circumvention" academy, so that upset folks too.

Okay, the attempt to dislodge me by using the auditors was unsuccessful. Next, a very unusual incident occurred. A man who worked for us in the Notasulga area asked me to meet him at his home. I agreed, and we set the date and time. Unsuspectingly, I drove to his home and knocked on the door. I was greeted not by the man but by his wife, who also worked for the schools, and she was dressed in a flimsy negligee. She invited me to come in to wait for her husband. I took one look and left her standing there. It seemed to me that I saw somebody out of my peripheral vision behind a garage or shed. I got in my car and got out of there as quickly as I could. I am satisfied that there were men ready to come into that house and catch me in a compromising situation. A few months later, both husband and wife resigned from their jobs in Macon County and moved away. So again, I suspected Wallace and his supporters trying to get rid of me.

Now, however, I became fearful that they would stop at nothing and that my family and I were not safe in Macon County.

It was also about this time that two women, Ann Buchanan and Mattie Perkins, began to picket the board of education offices. They would march up and down the sidewalk with signs for hours at a time. Ms. Buchanan was an employee of the board of education as a paraprofessional in the Title I program. She soon was seen driving a big new car. And she became a candidate for the board of education election that was coming up. The critics and naysayers all seemed to gravitate around her. At one board of education meeting, she got embroiled in an argument with Mr. Adams and one thing led to another until their confrontation became physical. Before anyone could stop him, Mr. Adams, who was the only white person on the board, had grabbed Ms. Buchanan's wrist. Well, we were able to calm Mr. Adams, but this confrontation became the *cause celebre* for Ms. Buchanan as the news spread.

As time for the election grew closer and the air of attacks grew more vicious, the board of education wanted to protect me by extending my contract beyond the current contract. Knowing that the attacks from the Wallace camp would not dissipate, I was actually ready to leave the state. Since I had told nobody about these events or my thinking, we agreed to let the election decide the issue.

Marilyn Pajot presenting scrapbook to Dr. Byas.

CHAPTER 6
Off to New York

Soon after I testified about the racist policies of the Alabama Educational Television station, I began to notice changes. State officials, who had previously been helpful and open with me, began not returning phone calls. Doors which had been open were now closed to Macon County school officials. These negative reactions on the part of state department of education officials were followed with harassing auditing by the state auditors, a process described in chapter 5. For more than a year, state auditors searched the books looking for any bit of evidence against me or the Macon County Board of Education that might be used in a legal case. None was ever found that could justify the time and taxpayers' expense that this search cost. The auditors were at our offices for so long that their paychecks were actually delivered to our offices! Also, the whole crisis with deliveries of gasoline occurred following my testimony, and I believe it was orchestrated by the Wallace supporters. Meanwhile, Dr. Frankie Ellis, who had also testified against the state educational television station, was manipulated into leaving Tuskegee Institute. The state threatened a holdup of funds that somehow ended after she was displaced. Dean Hunter coincidentally resigned and transferred to his alma mater, Iowa State University. It is my belief that he refused to fire Dr. Ellis and his departure was arranged by the same people who were harassing me. With Dean Hunter gone, they could get to Dr. Ellis.

As the efforts to dislodge me by means of the auditors proved futile, a small group of local protesters arose. A few people even began to picket our offices, carrying signs up and down the street outside the office. I expect this tactic was more unnerving to my subordinates and supporters who had no idea why the protest was going on than to me, because I did believe that it was motivated by the Wallace forces who wanted me out. In time, people noticed that two of the protest leaders, both women with limited incomes, were driving new luxury automobiles. It appeared obvious to me that funds were going into their pockets from an outside source. Again, the Wallace forces were suspected.

One of the protesters was Ann Buchanan, a paraprofessional in our Title I project. When she was elected to the school board several months later, she wanted to keep her job and hold her seat on the school board at the same time. State law, however, clearly prohibited school board members from working for the organization being supervised. Ms. Buchanan took her protest to court, but she lost her appeal.

These protests and the election of Ann Buchanan were public knowledge. But some of the things that happened were not, and I chose to keep them secret until many years later when I revealed the perniciousness of the attack on me to a select group of supporters during a visit to Tuskegee. One of the events that remained my secret was the apparent attempt to seduce me when I went, at an employee's invitation, to his home near one of our school campuses and was greeted by his wife in a flimsy negligee. I beat it out of there and was not surprised when that couple left the county. I believed that this attempt to lure me into a compromising situation was designed to get me beaten or killed. Or at the very least, it could be used as grounds for legal action to have me imprisoned for many years. It was this event that convinced me that my enemies were dangerous to my health and the safety of my family.

My supporters on the school board wanted to insulate me from the efforts of some within the community to remove me. Apparently, they thought that I could continue to serve the school community without strong support from the school board. Consequently, they offered me a renewed four-year contract. I saw it differently. I knew it would be an uphill battle to continue the improvements we had planned without strong board support, and I was becoming concerned for the political atmosphere and even wondering about the safety of my family and myself. I accepted a two-year extension of my contract with the proviso that if the newly constituted board wanted to remove me, I would have at least until July 1977.[1]

The new school board members, consisting of Dr. Evans Harris (chair), Kenneth Young (vice chair), Ann Buchanan, Clara Walker, and Allen Adams first met on November 22, 1976. During that meeting, a resolution was passed expressing the desire "to terminate the contract of the Superintendent and to work out with him, if possible, a mutually acceptable agreement."[2]

Mr. Adams resigned from the board shortly after the November 22 meeting. So on December 6, 1976, the board voted to end my contract after one year and additionally asked me to vacate my office on December 17, 1976, with the remaining six months to be paid me as a consultant as stipulated in my contract. I was also to be paid for consulting for an additional ninety-five days following the end of the contract year.[3] The board members attempted to dismiss me from the meeting at which my contract was discussed, but I persisted in remaining based on Alabama Code, Title 52.[4]

Actually, I was never consulted during that nine-month period, so I was able to concentrate my attention on finding a new position and moving my family. Some people wanted to help me find a job that would allow me to work three more years and become vested in the Alabama Teachers Retirement System, but I had no desire to do that under the circumstances. I was ready to get out of Alabama entirely.

Some of the employees of the Macon County School System provided me with a lovely send-off, not officially, of course, but at a private venue, on December 19. Dr. Meharry Lewis, JoAnn Wright, Wilhelmina Baldwin, Mary Bronson, Dr. Ellis Hall, Consuello Harper, Lucious Jefferson, Mary J. Lightfoot, Marilyn Pajot, and Lindsay Ray comprised the steering committee for the event. They honored me with a banquet at which several of my family members were in attendance, along with local supporters. They graciously gave me a scrapbook of letters and memorabilia and an oil painting of my visage. It was a warm-hearted effort, but none of those present knew the real reason for my leaving at the time. I just didn't believe it was the right time or place to lay that burden on them.

Well, one morning when I was going out to play golf, my wife Annamozel called me to the telephone and said it was long distance. The call was from a man that I did not know. He introduced himself as a superintendent of schools on Long Island, New York, who had agreed to be an unpaid consultant for the Roosevelt School District, which was looking for a superintendent. He wanted to know if I was available because he had talked to his friends in four states and my name had been mentioned. I said to him, "Well, I don't have a job, so yes, I'm available." He replied that he would give my name to the Roosevelt people.

They called about a week later, and I went for an interview. They called back and offered me the job, but I said, "No, I want a chance to look over the district at your expense before I make my decision." So they agreed to my conditions, providing a rental car and hotel for a week. I went to New York, went in and out of poolrooms, talked to people on the main drag, and basically looked things over without anyone knowing who I was. Nobody knew me, and I didn't know anybody either.

I decided to accept the job.

Even with moving expenses and a doubling of my Macon County salary, it was not much of an improvement because of the increased cost of living in New York. So no, it didn't pay much, but big pay has never been one of my criteria for taking a job. We were able to buy a house out of the salary and to live at the level to which we were accustomed.

Byas family at the unveiling of his portrait.

CHAPTER 7
Colleagues

Board Members

When I was hired in 1970, the county had recently elected three black members to the school board: Dr. P. K. Biswas, Dr. J. H. M. Henderson, and Dr. Ellis Hall, all of whom were professors at Tuskegee Institute. Mrs. Frances Rush, a white woman, was the board chair and resigned when the board voted to hire me, and Rev. Don Brown, pastor of the white United Methodist Church in Tuskegee resigned due to a transfer to another parish before I had an opportunity to work with him. The board replaced the minister with Mrs. Consuella Harper, a black woman activist from the Shorter community, and Mr. Allen Adams, a white businessman, was appointed by the board to replace Mrs. Rush. This newly constituted board also supported me in what I was attempting to do for the children of Macon County. They had the good sense to set the policies and leave the administration of daily affairs to me. Together, we were able to confront and resolve many of the problems facing the school system.

Mrs. Harper, who initially did not support my appointment, became a staunch supporter and led the board in publicly commending my work. Most board members became my good friends, especially Dr. Hall. He made his home available to me to have an eye-opening meeting with friends and supporters several years after I resigned from the Macon County Schools. It was here that I finally explained to these friends and associates what had occurred between the Wallace forces and me that led me to decline their kind offer of a four-year contract extension.

Over the years of my tenure, changes occurred in the composition of the board. Mr. Kenneth Young came on board in 1972, replacing Dr. Henderson. He was never a strong supporter of my vision. Then in 1976, Mrs. Ann Buchanan was elected as an outright opponent of my superintendency. It was shortly thereafter that I was asked to leave my position, and I willingly withdrew.

(In interviews conducted in 2003 with former school board members, this book's coauthor asked Dr. Hall, Dr. Henderson, and Mrs. Harper to comment on their experiences with Dr. Byas. Dr. Hall, who said he had been appointed to the board in 1969, said he was impressed with Byas's concerns for fiscal accountability at the time he was being interviewed. Hall, then a professor in the School of Veterinary Medicine, strongly supported Byas's policies. He said that when a problem arose, the superintendent would come to board meetings with plans and proposals to deal with the problem and that the board usually approved those plans and left him to carry out the necessary steps to accomplish the goals the board had set. As he looked back on Dr. Byas's tenure, he said he most regretted that the visionary plans for a vocational-technical school had never been carried forward after Byas left the area. He felt that was a truly shortsighted decision by the new board that deprived the children of Macon County of many opportunities. He also regretted that the board had not confronted the critics more directly when the first attacks were made on Dr. Byas's leadership.

Dr. Henderson, who served on the board from 1968 to 1972, was initially impressed with Byas's positive attitude, his background, and personality, making him an ideal candidate for the position and needs of the county. He remembered that Byas was very professional, always did his homework before coming to board meetings, and already had plans before they asked him questions. He had been particularly fond of the parenthood program, as well as the parenting aspect of the Title VIII program. In Dr. Henderson's words, the Macon County school system never recovered from the loss of Dr. Byas.

Mrs. Harper, the youngest board member during Byas's tenure, had very vivid and detailed memories of his work and the time period. Her own story is dramatic, having won a Ford Fellowship in Community Leadership as a leader in the West Macon Improvement Association, before starting a childhood-development program in Montgomery, Alabama. She reported on her confrontation with the previous superintendent, Joe Wilson, about the way the schools were failing the children of the county. This confrontation and her overall dissatisfaction with board policies led to her campaign to be elected to the school board. Elected in 1968, she served one term.

Initially she opposed Byas's hiring because she thought the board should hire someone from Macon County or at least from Alabama rather than someone from outside the area. A great concern of hers was the inequality between the opportunities for children in Tuskegee and the children in the rural areas. One of the things that helped win her over was his immediate understanding of the need to treat all areas of the county fairly. He was, she noted, "a tremendous visionary, a genius in his own right." She told him, "Go get your doctorate while I'm on this board. You already are one; you just need the papers." She described Byas as an innovator and an intellect.

According to Harper, many native Tuskegeeans saw Byas as being "outside their caste system," and these people were led by Ann Buchanan and Clara Walker. She noted that Buchanan threatened all of the board because she was uneducated and had no exposure to wider issues. They sensed that she was being paid because she had no job but suddenly had a new car. It was very suspicious.

Harper believes that the board failed the community by not educating the public better about the board's plans and need for visionary leadership. In this regard, she echoed words of Dr. Ellis. She said that she was not surprised when Dr. Byas decided to leave Macon County, and she was pleased that he found a more supportive environment in which to work.)

Staff Members I Inherited

Many of the staff members that were already working in Macon County when I arrived were excellent workers and outstanding supporters of my policies. These men and women had a thirst for progress and a strong desire to help the young people of their communities. They helped to make me look good in the eyes of the public with little or no recognition for their efforts. It gives me pleasure to acknowledge them in this manner, and while I am going to mention many names, I am confident that I will miss some persons who are equally deserving of praise.

Special acknowledgment is due to my secretary, Mrs. Bernice Nobles (now deceased). Some people wanted me to fire her because she was white. I did not. I said, "Let me see how well she does the job rather than to fire her because of her race and family members who support the segregation academy." I'm glad I made that decision, not only because it was the right and ethical thing to do but because she was an outstanding secretary. She would always be out of the office by four thirty, but everything I asked her to do would be completed and on my desk before she left. Since there was so much suspicion of some employees related to their support of the segregation academy, I instituted some policies to keep control of the mail, billing, and accounting, but she stepped right up and accepted the changes gracefully.

Several people deserve a lot of the credit for the writing of successful grant proposals. One key person was Martha Redhead. We would sit in my office and talk about the things we'd like to accomplish, and she and her staff were able to take my ideas and put them into a format that could be sold to governmental and nongovernmental agencies. As a result, Macon County Schools won several grants that helped to provide opportunities for our students that would otherwise have been impossible. Among their successful proposals were the Drop-Out Prevention Project (Title VIII) and the parenting program.

Mrs. Wilhelmina Baldwin, a veteran teacher and principal who initially opposed my appointment, became one of my greatest supporters and assets. I appointed her to head the curriculum and instruction department, and she did a tremendous job with it. Included in her work was the creation and supervision of a novel teacher/staff in-service program of mini-courses for all members of the staff, from the lunchroom workers and bus drivers to the school principals. She also helped to coordinate the observation and evaluation of teachers and the collection of information about curriculum improvement based on test results.

Our public relations messages were coordinated by Ernestine Sapp, who also wrote for the local newspaper. Walter Evans, principal of Tuskegee Public School, a property located in the heart of Tuskegee and adjacent to the office, was one of my first supporters. He took a lot of grief for doing so, and I looked upon him as a friend. In fact, I spoke about him at his funeral in 2006. Guy Crawford was willing to take on the challenge of serving as principal at the D. C. Wolfe High School and brought new programs to the students in Shorter. His talented wife, Jessie Crawford, took on the innovative piano-reading program, in which she took a bus loaded with electronic pianos around to the elementary schools and introduced music and reading concepts to primary school students. James Carter, a young and alert administrator, became the coordinator of the Title VIII program and showed much potential, going on to work with the Alabama Education Association after I left Macon County.

Staff That I Brought Onboard

One very creative gentleman who came to Macon County at my invitation was Jerry Hollingsworth. Jerry was a young white male who had worked with me when I was principal in Gainesville, Georgia. One of the things he supervised in Macon County was the school bus survey. He designed it, hired the students, and collated the resulting data, helping to make the decisions about bus stops, etc. He did this for two or three years before he moved out west with his new bride.

JoAnn Wright (now Haysbert) was probably the most persuasive young person I ever met. JoAnn was a bright attractive black woman who came to my office looking for a job right out of college. I asked her if she had a degree in education and she acknowledged that she did not. But she convinced me that she could do anything I needed that didn't require a teaching certificate. She became one of a cadre of young professionals in the research and development office, leaving our employ only to pursue a master's degree and doctorate in education. Ultimately, she came to her present position as president of Langston University. I made a good decision when I hired her.

Joann Wright, fall 1975.

Like Jerry Hollingsworth, Marilyn Pajot (now Robinson) came to Macon County after working with me in another capacity. She was director of research and publications with the Georgia Teachers and Education Association while I was associate executive secretary. We had worked together on several projects during the two years preceding the merger with the white Georgia Education Association. Marilyn was not averse to using her status as a white person and newcomer to Georgia to help the GTEA track down instances of discrimination against black educators. She also helped to document the loss of jobs when school desegregation led to jobs being offered to white band directors, principals, etc. and blacks being dismissed.

In Macon County, Marilyn worked with federal programs, starting as the parent counselor aid supervisor with the Drop-Out Prevention Project, then later as director of the piano-reading project and Title I parent coordinator. She also assisted with the research that led to my dissertation and was my first choice to cowrite this retrospective of my superintendency.

Finally, I hired an assistant superintendent, Mr. Lucious Jefferson, who helped to supervise many of the projects we initiated.

Civic Supporters

Among the civic supporters, I have to place Mayor Johnny Ford as number 1. He and the city council of Tuskegee, Alabama, worked with the school board on many projects. Through the Model Cities of Tuskegee organization, we were able to fund the construction of the Parenting Education center at Tuskegee Institute High School, for example.

NABSS

When the black teachers associations merged with their white counterparts across the South, black educators gained access to the mainstream organizations, but they lost the unique voice that the black associations had provided. In the vacuum left by the mergers, I conceived of the need for a new organization to speak for black educators.

Almost simultaneous to my tenure at Macon County Schools, Chuck Moody, then a student at Northwestern University who was working on a doctoral degree, asked Dr. Kenneth Clark, a nationally known black psychologist, to assist in getting funding to hold a meeting of several black school superintendents so he could do a survey for his dissertation. With Dr. Clark's support, a meeting was held at a motel near Chicago's O'Hare Airport, and it drew about fifteen of us, followed by a series of meetings four to five months apart. I was the only person in the group who came from the Deep South and, as such, was the only one who had had experience working with voluntary professional organizations, such as the Georgia Teachers and Education Association. I said to the others that while I was segregated *in,* they had been integrated *out* of leadership. Coming as they did from the Northeast, Midwest, and California, they had, at best, been on a committee. Almost none had even been chair of a committee, while I had been president and later assistant executive secretary of the GTEA. In fact, some of the members were afraid of speaking up and they advocated our group becoming an adjunct to the American Association of School Administrators rather than creating an independent organization. I made a speech which seems to have carried the day. It was titled "Me Speak for Me," and my goal was to convince them of the need for our own organization where we could set our own priorities and hold our own press conferences rather than holding a caucus and then going to a larger organization crying to hear our voice acknowledged. So the idea carried and the National Association of Black School Superintendents (NABSS) was formed. When we elected officers under the first charter, I was elected president, because I was the only one with prior experience.

It's ironic that at a time when Stokely Carmichael was preaching black power that the black teacher organizations were giving up power by merging with the larger white organizations. I had begun to think we made a mistake doing that. Now we had a new organization to fill that void.

Once we were organized, we wrote to the US commissioner of education within the Department of Health, Education, and Welfare (HEW) that we wanted to meet with him. (The US Department of Education was formed later.) By the time we met in New Orleans, we were still only thirty in number, but we got the commissioner to attend our meeting. I told the group, "Surely, he didn't come because of the number in the organization but because of the potential we had to grow. If we want to keep this potential going and keep the AASA from co-opting us, we need to increase our membership base." So for the whole of my tenure as president, I argued for the change in our name from NABSS to the NABSE (National Association of Black School Educators), which led to the change in our charter to include all classes of black educators, except teachers, as eligible for membership.

There was an additional clause that opened the membership to black teachers two years later. With these changes, the organization now has eight or nine thousand members. In my opinion, it should be more like 30,000 members, but some people were afraid that the organization would be run by the superintendents. I fought to have the organization democratized. I wanted to make sure the presidency did not fall only to superintendents, so our third president was not a superintendent and was a woman: Dr. Deborah C. Wolfe, formerly of Tuskegee.

Over the years, the organization has had its ups and downs, and I have been in and out and back in. Today, Chuck Moody is the recognized founder of the organization, but I believe I should be recognized as the cofounder and all of my efforts and documentation prove that. Nevertheless, I have decided to stay inactive rather than keep things stirred up.

All this organizing and meeting with colleagues around the country put me in touch with some people who have remained friends and supporters to this day, both members and others in national positions on the Education Commission: Hugh Scott, Sid Marlin, Dr. Townsel, and others. In fact, when I was struggling with my decision about testifying for the plaintiffs in the educational television case, it was a fellow superintendent and member of NABSS that I turned to for advice. And it was this organization that enabled me to build relationships that helped Macon County Schools to get some of the national grant money we so desperately needed.

I hope it's clear from this brief list that I had many supporters and helpers in tackling the problems of the Macon County School System, without whom my job would have been infinitely harder and much less successful. Those I've mentioned here are but examples of the many workers in the vineyard to whom I owe my thanks.

EPILOGUE

Byas and Macon County Schools after 1976

A few months before Dr. Byas was relieved of his responsibilities as superintendent of Macon County Schools, he was given an opportunity to speak at a banquet on July 16, 1976. He titled his speech "The Superintendency from a Black Perspective," and in his remarks, he spoke of the numerous challenges faced by black educators who are chosen to lead school systems.

> In school systems where a black is selected superintendent, one can see a string of problems characterized by financial indebtedness of the district, inadequate financial base, deteriorating buildings, insufficient printed materials and equipment, shifting population, complacency and/or hostile attitudes toward the school system by citizens, and low achievement of students as measured by standardized tests. All compounded by an extra large number of black and economically poor families.

In his remarks, he went on to describe the task of the black superintendent as similar to that faced by Moses when he led the Hebrew slaves out of Egypt toward the promised land. He raised the cry to stop treating blacks as "sick white people" and to find ways to provide equal opportunity for black students by understanding the sociology of the black family. He also raised the alarm about "metropolitanization" as a way to dilute the voting strength and leadership of blacks, and he asked if people really believe that blacks can create schools of quality and equality. In addition, he pointed out that opposition to the black superintendent was likely to come from two sources: racist whites and inexperienced grassroots persons who want to see immediate and dramatic changes without the pain of growth.

This address sums up much of Dr. Byas's experience and wisdom based on his tenure in Macon County. Fortunately, for education in general and black educational leadership, Dr. Byas's influence did not stop when he left Tuskegee. He continued his interactions with the University of Massachusetts, which conferred his doctorate, as a special lecturer for urban education in March of 1977, rating kudos from his supervisors.[1] He then went on to lead the Roosevelt school district in Long Island, New York, for ten years. He had such success that the district renamed a school after him following his retirement. It was a singular honor to a man who dedicated his life to educating youth in schools and church.[2]

Two letters summarize the feelings of many on his retirement from Roosevelt. R. Douglas Force wrote,

> I was a young man when Byas inspired me and other black children trapped in the corridors of inferior schools to seek knowledge and excellence, and for that deed, he was sentenced to be known among men as ULYSSES THE WANDERER, fated to cover the face of the earth, in search for a home.[3]

The other letter, from one of the people who initially opposed his coming to Macon County Schools, Wilhelmina F. Baldwin, compared Dr. Byas to "a turtle— not afraid to stick your neck out which you must do if you're going somewhere," and to "an eagle who soars high above the maze of problems and conflicts so that you can perceive the total picture."[4]

Following his retirement, Dr. Byas and his wife moved to Macon, Georgia, his birthplace, and settled into a routine of church, home, and family. He served as a founding member of the Middle Georgia chapter of Habitat for Humanity and served as the group's vice president. He also joined as an initial member of the Middle Georgia Alzheimer's Association and served on the board for seven years.

Accompanied by his extensive library of books and numerous file cabinets filled with the documents detailing his entire educational career, he has pursued every opportunity to continue telling his story and working for the improvement of educational opportunities for all. His creative mind is currently devoted to developing a number system for concepts.

In Tuskegee and Macon County, the changes are almost imperceptible since 1977. The school system did build a new comprehensive high school based on the plans written by Dr. Byas, but it did not build the vocational educational facility that Dr. Byas and his board of education had developed and hoped to build. The board halted plans to build this facility just thirty days before construction contracts were to be signed. The state of Alabama would have paid for the construction of the school and the salaries for ten teachers in perpetuity, had it been built in the 1970s as planned.

The new high school serves nearly all of the teenagers in Macon County with the exception of the Notasulga area. When, in 1990, it was proposed that all high school students would be required to attend the school, Notasulga, the community on the northern end of Macon County, objected to the plan and induced Dr. Byas to speak in their behalf at a hearing. Dr. Byas testified in the case of *Lee vs. Macon* to the progress made in Notasulga where the school had integrated in the early 1970s with success. He stated if the Notasulgans were forced to attend the new high school, the white student population would be so diluted as to lose their identity. Furthermore, the opportunity of black students in Notasulga to experience real integration would be lost. The community won and Notasulga continues to operate its own integrated high school, while the new high school serves the rest of the county, which is nearly 100 percent black.

Meanwhile, the white population of Tuskegee in particular continued to decrease, and in 1979 many businesses on Main Street were boarded up; only twenty-five persons attended the white United Methodist Church.[5]

A new shopping center was built in the 1980s as well as an industrial park with hopes of enticing growth. Mayor Johnny Ford continued to be reelected. The erection of a dog-racing track in the Shorter area garnered much support and provided many jobs and funds for new construction, including the building of the new high school.

Some dog-track proceeds were earmarked to address the problems in the county's public schools. In the mid-1980s, the Macon County Board of Education hired and then fired a series of school superintendents as it tried to reverse the perception that the schools generally were not fulfilling their purposes. The system suffered a high level of truancy and drug problems. A 1989 audit of the school board's operations found much income and spending unaccounted for. Increasingly, middle-class black families transported their children forty-five miles to private schools in Montgomery rather than send them to the local schools ... [6]

In the late 1990s, the optimism brought by the dog track had dissipated and new problems followed with the closing of the Wal-Mart and several other new businesses. In 1996, the long tenure of Mayor Ford was ended with the election of Ronald Williams.[7]

The struggles of black majorities to cope with the problems of self-government and education of their children continued to challenge the county. One can only hope that these challenges will be met as the years pass. Perhaps another person— man or woman—with the foresight and integrity of Ulysses Byas will appear to help lead the willing.

Ulysses Byas Elementary School, New York.
Dedicated on October 7, 2008.

Notes

Introduction

[1] Byas, *A Proposal*, 1.
[2] Norrell, 3.
[3] Ibid., 9.
[4] Ibid., 10.
[5] Ibid., 12–13.
[6] Ibid., 20–21.
[7] Ibid., 22.
[8] Ibid., 30.
[9] Ibid., 25.
[10] Ibid., 31–36.
[11] Ibid., 46–47.
[12] Ibid., 53.
[13] Ibid., 59.
[14] Ibid., 65–75.
[15] Byas, *A Proposal ... Appendix* 1.
[16] Norrell, 77–80.
[17] Ibid., 81–85.
[18] Ibid., 86–88.
[19] Ibid., 88–90.
[20] Ibid., 93–95.
[21] Ibid., 96–102.
[22] Ibid., 96–99.
[23] Ibid., 100.
[24] Ibid., 102–107.
[25] Ibid., 110–120.
[26] Ibid., 120–126.
[27] Ibid., 128–131.
[28] Ibid., 137–139.
[29] Ibid., 140–141.

[30] Ibid., 144–146.
[31] Ibid., 148–150.
[32] Ibid., 151–159
[33] Ibid., 160–161.
[34] Ibid., 164–165.
[35] Ibid., 165–167.
[36] Ibid., 168.
[37] Ibid., 168–178.
[38] Ibid., 178–184.
[39] Ibid., 184–191.
[40] Ibid., 191–198.
[41] Ibid., 198–200.

Chapter 1

[1] *Gainesville Times*, undated clipping.
[2] *Tuskegee Progressive Times*, June 25, 1970.
[3] Ibid.
[4] Tindley.
[5] *Hamlet*, act 4, scene 5.
[6] Adams (chapter 11), 314.
[7] Walker, Vanessa Sidle.

Chapter 3

[1] News release, January 19, 1973.
[2] News release, February 1, 1972.
[3] The Auburn Center, 1971; Alabama State Board of Education, 1972; Blue Ribbon Citizens' Committee, 1978.

Chapter 4

[1] Excerpts from superintendent's address, August 26, 1971.
[2] Macon County Board of Education, February 3, 1971.
[3] Interview, June 21, 2002.
[4] *Your Macon Education Reporter*, May 1972.
[5] Byas, 1976; Macon County Board of Education, July 17, 1973.
[6] Macon County Board of Education, December 15, 1971.

[7] Ibid.
[8] Interview, June 21, 2002.
[9] Macon County Board of Education, January 1976.
[10] Interview, June 21, 2002.
[11] Macon County Board of Education, June 1972.
[12] Macon County Board of Education, June 1972, 10.
[13] From a speech given on January 30, 1975.

Chapter 5

[1] FCC 74–1385, 10.
[2] FCC 74–1385, 15–17.

Chapter 6

[1] Letter, March 23, 1976, to MCBOE.
[2] Special board meeting minutes, December 1, 1976.
[3] Letter, November 29, 1976, to MCBOE, and agreement signed December 1, 1976.
[4] Open letter, *Tuskegee News*, December 16, 1976.

Epilogue

[1] Memorandum, March 29, 1977.
[2] *Newsday*, February 27, 2002.
[3] Letter from Douglas Force.
[4] Letter from Wilhelmina F. Baldwin, March 26, 1987.
[5] Norrell, 209.
[6] Ibid., 210–211.
[7] Ibid., 213–216.

Bibliography

Introduction

Byas, Ulysses. *A Proposal to Demonstrate the Feasibility of Establishing a Comprehensive Community Facility.* Macon County (Alabama) Board of Education. Undated.

Norrell, Robert J. *Reaping the Whirlwind: The Civil Rights Movement in Tuskegee.* The University of North Carolina Press, Chapel Hill, North Carolina. 1998.

Chapter 1

Adams, Henry. *The Education of Henry Adams: A Biography.* Boston: Houghton Mifflin, 1918.

Byas, Ulysses. Letter to Rep. Floyd B. Hicks. November 27, 1972.

Byas, Ulysses and Marilyn V. Pajot. "The Displacement of African American Teachers and Principals." *Georgia Teachers and Education Association Herald.*

"Byas Leaving Great Loss." *The Daily Times* (Gainesville, Georgia). May 23, 1968.

Gainesville Times. Undated.

Tindley, Charles Albert. "Leave It There." 1916 (song, public domain).

Tuskegee Progressive Times. June 25, 1970.

Rangel, Charles B. Letter to Ulysses Byas. February 27, 1973.

Roy. Letter to Ulysses Byas. May 21, 1968.

Shakespeare, William. *Hamlet.*

Chapter 2

Alabama Bill H.2183 as signed by Gov. George Wallace. September 20, 1971.

"Appointment of Superintendent Draws Fire." *Tuskegee Progressive Times.* June 4, 1970.

Blair, J. C. Letter to Ulysses Byas. June 3, 1970. Ulysses. News release. Undated.

Bowler, Mike. "Tuskegee Gets Negro Superintendent." *Atlanta Constitution.* June 9, 1970.

Byas, Ulysses. Letter to Model Cities Members (with attachment). May 16, 1972.

Byas, Ulysses. "Memorandum re: Gasoline Purchasing Consolidation Proposal (with addendum)." April 10, 1973.

Byas, Ulysses. "Memorandum re: Loan Payments." Undated.

"Byas Accepts Position …" *Tuskegee Progressive Times.* June 4, 1970.

Education Association of Macon. Telegram to Ulysses Byas. May 29, 1970.

"Ex-Butler Principal May Be First Negro Superintendent in SE." *Gainesville* (Georgia) *Times.* Undated.

Macon County Board of Education. Flyers for Tax Vote. Undated.

Macon County Board of Education. "Macon County Public Schools Heavily Dependent on Federal Funds." News release. Undated.

Macon County Board of Education. "Macon County Public School Taxes, 1967–1973."

"No Fees for School." *Macon Education Reporter.* June 1971.

Macon County Board of Education. Minutes of board of education meeting. January 24, 1973.

Macon County Board of Education. "Per Pupil Cost by School for Gas for Heating and Cooking, Electric and Water for Month of February 1973."

Macon County Board of Education. "School Bus Survey." April 1977.

Macon County Board of Education. "Student Enrollment, Faculty Employed in 1969–70."

Macon County Board of Education. "Student Enrollment, Teachers and Aides by School and Race, Bus Drivers and Office Staff." January 29, 1971.

Macon County Board of Education. "Support of Public School Education in Macon County." September 1976.

Macon County Board of Education. "Trends in Macon County Public School Enrollment." 1971.

Meyer, Sylvan. "Success Story of Ulysses Byas." *Miami News.* Undated.

Nordheimer, Jon. "Negro Will Head Tuskegee Schools." *New York Times.* June 10, 1976.

Perry, Harmon. "White Exodus Bothers Black: Negro School Boss." *The Atlanta Journal.* July 30, 1970.

Rush, Frances. Letter to Ulysses Byas. June 8, 1970.

Sapp, Ernestine. "Byas Will Strive to Work with All People." *Tuskegee Progressive Times.* June 25, 1970.

Sapp, Ernestine. "School Board Answers Questions about Superintendent." *Tuskegee Progressive Times.* June 11, 1970.

State Department of Education (Alabama). "Table of Income and Revenue by Counties." July 6, 1970.

State of Alabama. "Report of a Partial Survey of Macon County School System: School Year 1971–1972." 1972.

Alabama State Board of Education. "School Survey Series No. 292." 1972.

The Auburn Center. "Macon County Schools: 1971." Auburn University. June 1971.

Blue Ribbon Citizens' Committee. "Final Report," May 1, 1978.

Byas, Ulysses. "Guidelines for the Design of a Comprehensive High School for Macon County, Alabama: Dream." September 1974.

Byas, Ulysses. Letter. March 26, 1973.

Macon County Board of Education. "A Summary of Some Improvements Made and Planned for Immediate Future throughout the School System." October 19, 1971.

_____. "Building Cleanliness Report by School." February 1971.

_____. News release. February 1, 1972.

_____. News release. January 19, 1973.

_____. "Confidential Draft." Undated.

Wallace, George C. Letter to Ulysses Byas. March 1, 1972.

Byas, Ulysses. "A Study of Some Residual Effects of a Temporary Dropout Prevention Program on Participating Parents and Students Located in a Disadvantaged and Majority Black School District." Doctoral dissertation. University of Massachusetts: 1976.

Byas, Ulysses. "Our Responsibility." Undated.

Byas, Ulysses. Speech. January 30, 1975.

Macon County Board of Education. Appraisal sheet for classroom observation. 1973.

_____. "Board of Education Implements New Projects." Undated.

_____. Dropout Prevention Project grant proposal. February 3, 1971.

_____. Evaluation and Test Analysis of the Fourth Grade Reading Program. June 1972a.

_____. Final Evaluation Report of Project ARISE. July 17, 1973.

_____. "Lewis Adams Receives Accreditation." News release. Undated.

_____. News release. December 15, 1971.

_____. Program Evaluation: Preparation for Parenthood and Early Childhood Development, 1971–74. August 1974.

_____. Request of Support from the Spencer Foundation, January 1976.

_____. Results of Cureton Reading Program as Implemented in Grades Five and Six. June 1972b.

Your Macon Education Reporter. May 1972.

Agress, Ellen S. Letter. January 9, 1975.

Baxley, Williams J., Attorney General. Letter. August 9, 1976.

Brown, LeRoy. Letter. January 13, 1975.

Burson, B. M. Letter. April 24, 1974.

Byas, Ulysses. Affidavit. January 3, 1973.

Paper, Lewis J. Letter. December 21, 1972.

Rush, Frances H. Letter. May 21, 1970.

State of Alabama, The Alabama Educational Television Network. "Approaching—Total Communications Service for All Alabamians." Undated pamphlet.

_____. Audit Report of the Macon County Board of Education. November 5, 1976.

_____. Department of Examiners of Public Accounts Report of Examination of Macon County, Alabama, October 1, 1973 through September 30, 1974.

_____. Department of Examiners of Public Accounts. County Board of Education, Macon County, Alabama October 1, 1976 through September 30, 1978. March 26, 1980.

United States Federal Communications Commission 74–1385.

Macon County Board of Education. "A Tribute to Dr. Ulysses Byas." December 19, 1976.

Byas, Ulysses and Annamozel Byas. Letter to Ellis Hall. May 17, 2000.

Macon County Board of Education. Dedication of Deborah Cannon Wolfe School Addition. April 14, 1974.

"Notasulga PTA Honors Supt. Byas at Meet." *The Tuskegee News*. April 4, 1974.

Baldwin, Wilhelmina F. Letter. March 26, 1987.

Byas, Ulysses. Speech: The Superintendency from a Black Perspective. July 16, 1976.

Memorandum. March 29, 1977.

Newsday. February 27, 2002.

Norrell, Robert J. *Reaping the Whirlwind: The Civil Rights Movement in Tuskegee.* Chapel Hill, North Carolina: The University of North Carolina Press. 1998.

Scott, Hugh J. *The Black School Superintendent: Messiah or Scapegoat.* Washington, DC: Howard University Press, 1980.

Walker, Vanessa Siddle with Ulysses Byas. *Hello Professor: A Black Principal and Professional Leadership in the Segregated South.* Chapel Hill, North Carolina: The University of North Carolina Press, 2009.

APPENDIX

Some Documents Related to the Work of Ulysses Byas in Macon County, Alabama.

```
OUR   RESPONSIBILITY   AS   A   PUBLIC   SCHOOL   DISTRICT   IS   TO

               EDUCATE   ALL   CHILDREN

CHILDREN FROM TWO PARENT HOMES, ONE PARENT HOMES, OR THOSE
      CHILDREN FROM HOMES WITH NO PARENT AT ALL

         CHILDREN FROM SPACIOUS, EXPENSIVE HOMES;
            OR CRAMPED, DILAPIDATED HOMES.

CHILDREN FROM MORTGAGED HOMES, RENTED HOMES, WELFARE HOMES,
FOSTER HOMES OR ORPHANAGE HOMES. CHILDREN FROM CARING HOMES,
SHARING HOMES, SUPPORTIVE HOMES, SELFISH HOMES OR ENVIOUS
HOMES. CHILDREN FROM EDUCATIONALLY CHEATED HOMES, HOMES WITH
UNEMPLOYMENT AND OR UNDEREMPLOYMENT.

   CHILDREN FROM EDUCATED HOMES, LOVING  HOMES, GOOD HOMES;
       ILLITERATE HOMES, LONELY HOMES, BROKEN HOMES OR
            CHILDREN FROM NO HOME AT ALL.

CHILDREN! COME! SHORT OR TALL, THIN OR PLUMP, DISADVANTAGED
OR GIFTED, PLANE OR HANDSOME, SPECIAL OR NORMAL, DRAMATIC OR
ATHLETIC, POETIC OR MUSICAL. CHILDREN! COME! WILLFUL OR
FORCED, STUDIOUS OR LAZY, INTELLIGENT OR DULL, QUESTFUL OR
QUESTLESS, FORCEFUL OR SHY, LAWFUL OR LAW-BREAKER.
         IT REALLY MAKES NO DIFFERENCE!  COME!

      OUR CHARGE AS A PUBLIC SCHOOL DISTRICT IS TO
                EDUCATE ALL CHILDREN!
         WHETHER IN EXPENSIVE DESIGNER CLOTHES OR
              THRIFT SHOP SPECIALS. COME!

by: ulysses byas
```

Ulysses Byas's credo.

Macon County Board of Education
Tuskegee, Alabama 36083
June 8, 1970

Mr. Ulysses Byas
201 Ashby Street, N.W.
Atlanta, Georgia 30314

Dear Mr. Byas:

We were pleased to receive your letter of acceptance dated 26 May 1970 for the position of Superintendent of Education of Macon County.

We have made a public announcement in the two local newspapers, The Tuskegee News and The Tuskegee Progressive Times (see enclosed clipping from the latter).

At an announced (see NOTICE) public meeting last Friday evening at the Tuskegee Public School, we informed the public of your acceptance and read your credentials to them (there were approximately 400 people present).

I believe we can say that the public generally warmly endorses and welcomes your appointment.

You indicated in your letter the willingness to meet with Mr. Harvey and the Board to discuss personnel assignments and other plans for the coming school year. We would hope that possibly the week of the 15th would be convenient to accomplish the above; if not, the week of the 22nd.

In addition, I assume you will want to be looking into housing, on which Dr. Hall has been confering with you. In this connection I presume you and your wife both would like to come to Tuskegee to do some "house hunting."

Arrangements can be made for your staying at the campus guest house, Dorothy Hall, or if you prefer, at a Holiday Inn, but the nearest one is about 25 miles away.

We look forward to hearing from you at your earliest convenience You may feel free to call, if you so desire.

Sincerely yours,

Frances H. Rush

(Mrs.) Frances H. Rush, Chairman
Macon County Board of Education

cc: Mr. Alonza Harvey
    Board of Education Members

Letter appointing Ulysses Byas to the office of Macon County Superintendant of Schools. See p. 37.

Telegram

727P EDT MAY 29 70 AA386 NSB340   IB CFM D OFC
NS LLM582 BA PD JB TUSKEGEE ALA 29 527P CDT
ULYSEES BYAS   DA 834P EW
  201 ASHBY ST NORTHWEST GEORGIA TEACHERS ASSN ATLA 3031-
THE PEOPLE OF TUSKEGEE AND MACON COUNTY ARE AWARE OF THE FACT
THAT YOU HAVE MADE APPLICATION TO THE BOARD OF EDUCATION FOR
THE POSITION OF SUPERINTENDENT OF MACON COUNTY SCHOOLS.
THE PEOPLE OF TUSKEGEE AND MACON COUNTY ARE ALSO AWARE THAT
ACTING AS SUPERINTENDENT AT PRESENT IS MR ALONZO HARVEY A GENTLEMAN
WHO HAS LIVED IN MACON COUNTY AND WHO HAS SERVED THE CAUSE
OF EDUCATION IN MACON COUNTY FOR THE PAST DECADE. HE IS DOING
AN ADMIRABLE JOB AS ACTING SUPERINTENDENT ALTHOUGH HE WAS EXPLOITED
TO ASSUME THIS ROLE. HE HAS COME UP THROUGH THE RANKS, AND
HE IS THE MAN OUR PEOPLE REALLY WANT AND PLEDGE TO SUPPORT   Pg. 1
AS SUPERINTENDENT.
120ALL TEACHERS, PRINCIPALS, CENTRAL OFFICE PERSONNEL, BUS DRIVERS
  AND SCHOOL SHOP EMPLOYEES HAVE INDICATED IN WRITING THAT THEY
  ARE PROUD OF THE JOB THAT MR HARVEY HAS DONE AND THEREFORE
  URGE THE BOARD TO APPOINT HIM.
  IN ADDITION TO THIS TYPE OF SUPPORT THERE ARE SEVERAL HUNDRED
  SIGNATURES FROM PEOPLE IN THE COMMUNITY SUPPORTING THE FACT
  THAT MR ALONZO HARVEY SHOULD BE APPOINTED SUPERINTENDENT.
  WE FEEL THAT IF YOU ARE MADE AWARE OF THE TREMENDOUSLY STRONG
  SUPPORT IN WRITING WHICH WE HAVE ON HAND FOR MR HARVEY'S APPOINTMENT
  YOU WOULD WANT TO PROMPTLY WITHDRAW YOUR APPLICATION AT THIS
  TIME SO THAT SMOOTH PROGRESSION OF EDUCATIONAL ACTIVITIES MAY
  CONTINUE IN MACON COUNTY.   Pg. 2
  WE SOLICIT YOUR PROFESSIONAL COOPERATION AND HOPE TO HEAR FROM
  YOU DIRECTLY.   7
SF-120SINCERELY YOURS
     EDUCATION ASSN OF MACON
     PO BOX 90 TUSKEGEE ALA 36083
     CARE MR CYRUS WILLIS.   Pg. 3

     90 36083.(619)

Telegram opposing appointment of Byas as superintendent.

Documents related to the administration of Macon County Schools.

A summary of Some Improvements Made and Planned for Immediate Future
Throughout the School System.

I. SCHOOL REPAIRS
   School Plant Renovation:
   A. $213,000.00 contract with Lockard Construction Company for:

   a. Lewis Adams School - connection of new building to city sewer;
      new wiring; fixtures and new roof on old building and repair
      of windows.

   b. Tuskegee Public School - new roof and gutter work on main
      building and repair of plumbing.

   c. Washington Public School - new floor in old building, new
      plumbing, painting and repair of windows.

   d. Tuskegee Institute High School - Rewiring and new fixtures
      in old building and new ceiling, walls and floors through-
      out except gym; repair of windows. New doors at main en-
      trance.

The above work was made possible by a $176,000.00 grant from the Tuskegee
Model Cities Program. The remainder of funds came from the State of Alabama.

   B. $66,000.00 worth of work has been completed since this summer
      or is under contract.

   a. Prairie Farms - Painting the exterior and repair of porch
      and roofing and replacing septic field.

   b. Shorter - renovate house for Exceptional Program; one room
      in gym; ordered one three classroom mobile unit.

   c. South Macon - repainted the interior of old building with
      Apoxy paint and replaced the coal burner with fuel oil
      system; one three classroom mobile unit.

   d. Notasulga High - Painting of building exterior; replace
      septic field; one three classroom mobile unit.

   e. Nichols Junior High - one three classroom mobile unit.

   f. Children House - Labor for repainting kitchen and cafeteria
      and replacement of windows.

   g. D. C. Wolfe High - Improved water supply system.

The above work was made possible through local, Title I, and state funds.
Other work planned for this year is inclusive of, but not necessarily,
limited to the following: repainting interior of D. C. Wolfe High, Shorter,
and Tuskegee Public. Roof repairs at Tuskegee Public, South Macon, Nichols,
Institute High and Notasulga High. Toilet repairs at Tuskegee Public, Notasulga, Children House and South Macon. New floors at Tuskegee Public, Institute High and Lewis Adams.

II. DROPOUTS

Title VIII: $150,000.00 program working toward dropout prevention, twenty-four parents are employed at a salary of $360.00 per month. There are five staff persons working with this program.

III. ATTENDANCE

Preparation for Parenthood and Early Childhood Development Program; $184,813.00 for the construction of a building and first year operation of a program designed to aid young girls with babies under thirty months and who are expecting a child and to continue their high school careers. Target date for program operation is November 15, 1971.

The above program was made possible through a $55,000.00 grant for building construction from Tuskegee Model Cities and a $129,813.00 operational grant from United States Department of Health, Education and Welfare.

IV. INSTRUCTION:

Instructional Supplies: $25,000.00 for purchasing of supplies to aid in the instructional program. This has enabled the Board to prohibit fund raising activities and snack bars of any kind as well as to eliminate charging of fees of any kind except typing.

The above program was made possible through state and local funds.

V. STAFF:

Support staff at Institute High: $33,800.00 for the addition of two guidance counselors, one assistant principal and two secretaries.

The above was made possible through local and federal funds.

VI. BANDS, READING, NEWSPAPER, DATA

Emergency School Assistance: $225,000.00 application which is pending for the establishment of a band program at Notasulga, D. C. Wolfe and South Macon Schools and the purchase of musical instruments at Institute High and Tuskegee Public. The publication of four editions of system newspaper; establishment of data collection, storage and retrieval system; development of model reading program at fifth and sixth grade levels.

This proposal is under consideration by Regional Office of Education in Atlanta. We expect to hear from them on October 22, 1971.

VII. READING

Development of and installation of a model reading program at the fourth grade level throughout the school system. Three persons are employed in this program which is funded by the Tuskegee Model Cities Program in the amount of $25,000.00.

VIII. FINANCES:

In spite of the fact that no money has come from the state, the
Board of Education has managed to meet most of its financial
obligation without borrowing any money. This has been made
possible by delaying some payments and watching very closely
every penny spent.

IX. TEXTBOOKS:

We have had a very poor accounting system of textbooks at best at
both the central office and the school levels. This situation is
improving rapidly. We have found instances where teachers preferred
another book and did not issue any, even though, there were enough
on hand. During the past fourteen months we have purchased and
delivered to the several schools $19,000.00 worth of new books for
grades eight through twelve. Our areas of greatest need at this
time appears to be in grades: five, six, seven and in a few areas
in high school. With a budget this year and proper accounting at
the school level this matter of shortage should clear up completely.

In this news release, Byas explained in detail the fact that most of the school funding came from the federal government, not from local taxes.

MACON COUNTY BOARD OF EDUCATION

NEWS RELEASE

MACON COUNTY PUBLIC SCHOOLS HEAVILY DEPENDENT ON FEDERAL FUNDS

Last year Macon County Board of Education spent approximately $5,165,000. "Of this," says Superintendent Ulysses Byas, "some $3,171,000 was derived from Federal sources. This represents 61% of the total school budget for last year." (The National average is about 7%.)

"An additional $1,795,000," continued Byas, "came from State funds. This made up some 35% of the total budget. $199,000, or 4%, came from local revenue."

The $5,165,000 budget, which included all but purely local school monies such as PTA funds, athletic funds, and non-federal lunchroom funds, reflects revenue from some 20 different federal programs or agencies.

"Even more federal money is expected this year," explained Byas. "With the Title VIII Project, the Planned Parenthood Program and an increase in the Emergency School Assistance allocation, the Federal share will increase from 61% to about 64%, a total of some $3,525,252 for 1971-72 school year."

Mr. Byas explained that no major increases in State or local monies were anticipated.

Expected sources of Federal money for 1971-72 are:

Title I ESEA	$641,776
Title II ESEA	7,521
Title III NDEA	14,922
Career Opportunities Program	98,756
Follow Through	662,980
Head Start	436,076
Adult Basic Education	15,440
Neighborhood Youth Corp(out-of-school)	132,865
Neighborhood Youth Corp(in-school and summer)	238,477
Special Education - Title VI	17,211
Emergency School Assistance Program	128,878
Educational Development Center	100,000
United State Department of Agriculture	233,187
ROTC	24,245
Drivers Education	4,636
Tuskegee Model Cities	271,826
Vocational Education	74,389
Bank Street	19,322
Commodities (USDA)	61,889
Public Law 874 - Impacted Areas	105,976
Forestry Service	1,068
Title VIII	149,000
Prep. Planned Parenthood + Childhood Development	184,813

1971-72 GRAND TOTAL $ 3,525,252

103

Expected 1971-72 State Revenue will be about $1,795,000 and Local Revenue about $200,000. This totals a 5½ million dollar budget for 1971-72.

"What this means," said Superintendent Byas, "is that, as a average, we will spend $938 per student in programs operated by the Board; $599 of this will be Federal funds, $305 will be State funds, and $34 will be local funds."

"In other words," pointed out Superintendent Byas, "if we only had local money available we would operate, at the present level, an educational system for about 200 students; were only State and Local money available we could operate our system at its present level for only about 2125 students. Thanks in part to Federal money we now operate a system for nearly 6000 students rangeing from Head Start through Adult Basic Education classes."

"Relatively speaking the Federal share of the school budget increases while the State and Local shares decrease," concluded Byas. "That warrants the attention of all parents and interested community members in our county."

PLEASE Post

MACON COUNTY BOARD OF EDUCATION
TUSKEGEE, ALABAMA 36083

PER PUPIL COST BY SCHOOL FOR GAS FOR HEATING AND COOKING - ELECTRIC
AND WATER FOR MONTH OF JANUARY, 1973.

1. SCHOOL	2. NO. STUDENTS ENROLLED	3. GAS BILL	4. AVG. COST PER PUPIL	5. ELECTRIC WATER SEWAGE GARBAGE	6. AVG. COST PER PUPIL	7. TOTAL COST UTILITIES	8. AVG. TOTAL COST UTILITIES
Chambliss	223					$ 372.00	$ 1.67
D. C. Wolfe	344			$ 185.75	$ .54	185.75	.54
Lewis Adams	497	$ 368.00	$ .74	320.76	.65	688.76	1.39
Nichols	303	306.06	1.01	141.96	.47	448.02	1.48
Notasulga	516	623.62	1.21	330.54	.64	954.16	1.85
Prairie Farms	221			116.63	.53	116.63	.53
Shorter	337	504.17	1.50	125.22	.37	629.39	1.87
South Macon	701	476.87	.68	233.64	.33	710.51	1.01
Institute High	930	777.42	.84	1,034.51	1.11	1,811.93	1.95
Tuskegee Public	620	675.14	1.09	331.35	.53	1,006.49	1.62
Washington Public	463	372.99	.81	303.10	.65	676.09	1.46
TOTALS	5155	$4,476.27	.87	$3,123.46	.61	$7,599.73	$ 1.47

NOTE: To All Personnel

The $7,599.73 listed in column 7 is the total cost of utilities for the month of January. This figure does not include the cost of coal for Prairie Farms nor the cost of fuel oil for D. C. Wolfe and South Macon Schools. The bill this month represents approximately a $2,000.00 increase caused by changes in utilities rates.

Gasoline for the operation of buses is costing us .04¢ per gallon more over the previous month. Last year we purchased 130,000 gallons of gasoline.

MACON COUNTY BOARD OF EDUCATION

MACON COUNTY PUBLIC SCHOOL TAXES

* Local Funds

YEAR	ENROLLMENT	TOTAL MONEY RECEIVED THROUGH LOCAL TAXES	YEARLY AMOUNT SPENT PER PUPIL FROM LOCAL TAXES	MONTHLY AMOUNT SPENT PER PUPIL FROM LOCAL TAXES	DAILY AMOUNT SPENT PER PUPIL FROM LOCAL TAXES
1967-68	5,666	101,436.92	17.91	1.99	.11
1968-69	5,562	105,097.71	18.88	2.10	.11
1969-70	5,542	185,373.89	33.45	3.72	.19
1970-71	5,259	192,013.88	36.52	4.06	.21
1971-72 **	5,285	203,038.10	38.43	4.27	.22
1972-73	5,253	208,616.38	39.72	4.42	.23

* Money received by the County and District Taxes for support of Public Education.
** Pupil expenditures from Local Taxes for Counties surrounding Macon County, 1971-72

Lee	5,004	630,288.42	125.96	14.00	.72
Russell	4,717	223,359.84	47.36	5.27	.27
Tallapoosa	3,729	389,635.61	104.49	11.61	.60
Montgomery	39,455	1,685,721.58	42.75	4.75	.25
Bullock	2,700	100,385.51	43.38	4.81	.25

106

MACON COUNTY BOARD OF EDUCATION
Post Office Box 90
TUSKEGEE, ALABAMA 36083

March 26, 1973

MR. ULYSSES BYAS
SUPERINTENDENT

Dear

As you know the Macon County Board of Education operates eleven schools in our system. All of our buildings, with one exception, are of permanent type construction and are, in a sense, modern. Our Prairie Farms facility which has an enrollment of approximately 275 students, Head Start through the third grade, all of which reside in the western part of the county.

If you have not visited the Prairie Farms campus we urgently invite you to do so at your earliest convenience. You will find a series of old frame buildings of which we have, through the years, made emergency repairs. The heating system utilizes old pot-bellied stoves and is probably the only such building in Alabama. Our lunch room and food preparation area are very much below standards. The site is of such that puddles of water stand literally for days after each and every rain.

Because of the above enumerated items, among others, we have employed an architect who is developing plans which, when implemented, will add an addition to the D. C. Wolfe High School thus making it possible to abandon the Prairie Farms facility.

The D. C. Wolfe High School does not have a kitchen and cafeteria. Because of this deficiency, we have transported students daily to the Shorter Elementary School, which has limited facilities, for lunches. In our collective judgement the decision was made to build one addition at a site which would solve this and the Prairie Farm problem.

We are planning a twelve classroom addition plus a lunchroom. We have been told by our architect that such a project would cost $300,000.00. We have in our current budget $200,000.00. We are in need of an additional $100,000.00 so that this project could move forward immediately. We urgently and respectfully request the County Commission to give us this amount of money for this much needed project.

We will be happy to come to your meeting to explain any details in connection with this project which you may desire.

Thanking you so very much for whatever consideration you may give, I am

Sincerely yours,

P. K. Biswas, Chairman
Board of Education

Ulysses Byas, Superintendent

UB/bn

The addition to the Deborah Cannon Wolfe
High School on the day of dedication,
April 14, 1974.

PREPARAT... FOR PARENTHOOD AND
EARLY CHILDHOOD DEVELOPMENT

TAB. 4

ANNUAL SITUATIONAL VARIABLES

END OF PROGRAM YEAR SITUATION	1971 - 1972	1972 - 1973	1973 - 1974
PREGNANCIES	25	20	15
LIVE BIRTHS	22	20	13
MISCARRIAGES	3	0	2
STILL BIRTHS	0	0	0
MOTHERS WITH CHILDREN PRIOR TO PROGRAM ENTRY	29	41	35
RECIDIVISM	0	1	0
TOTAL NUMBER OF PARTICIPANTS	54	61	50

29

Program Evaluation: Preparation for Parenthood and Early Childhood Development
#1971-1974. Aug 1974, Tuskegee, AL

109

MACON COUNTY BOARD OF EDUCATION
P. O. BOX 90
TUSKEGEE, ALABAMA 36083

February   1971

MONTHLY BUILDING CLEANLINESS REPORT BY SCHOOL

SCHOOLS	GROUNDS	HALLWAYS	WINDOWS & BLINDS	KITCHEN	STORAGE	CAFETERIA	GYM.	R.O.T.C.	OTHER	CLASSROOMS 1	2	3	4	5	6	HEAD START	TOILETS 1	2	3	4	5	GENERAL APPEARANCE	CLINIC	AUDITORIUM	VOC. AGR.	HOME MAKE	POINTS EARNED	MAXIMUM POINTS	PERCENTAGE
PRAIRIE FARMS	8	8	6	6	8			?		7						7	8					6	8				72	90	80
TUSKEGEE PUBLIC	9	7	6	9	6	9				6	6	6	6	6	6		6	7	6	6		6	8			7	126	162	77
C. C. HOUSE	7	7	6	7	6	7	6	?		6							6					6	6				70	99	71
NICHOLS JR. HIGH	6	8	6	6	6	6		?		6							6					6	6				62	90	69
SOUTH MACON	6	6	6	6	6	6				6	6						6	6				6	6		6	7	85	126	67
WASHINGTON PUBLIC	6	6	6	6	5	7				6	6						5	6				6	6				71	108	66
SHORTER ELEMENTARY	5	7	5	6	6	6	5			6							6					6	6				64	99	65
NOTASULGA HIGH	6	6	6	6	5	7	(2)		6	6	6						(2)	5	6	6		6	6	6	6		99	162	61
TUSKEGEE INST. HIGH	7	7	4	6	5	6	5		5	6	6	6	6				4	4	4	4	6	6	6	6			109	180	61
LEWIS ADAMS	4	6	4	(5)	6	6			?	6	6	6					5					6	6				66	117	56
D. C. WOLFE	(3)	6	(2)		6		5			(3)	6	(3)					3					(4)			(3)	(3)	47	108	44

SCALE

81 - 100 Excellent   80 - 61 Very Good
60 - 41 Good   40 - 21 Fair
        0 - 20 Poor

110

MACON COUNTY BOARD OF EDUCATION
Tuskegee, Alabama

Appraisal sheet for classroom observation (1973)

Section G, item 9 of the Policy Manual of the Macon County Board of Education states, "The principal shall make at least three formal observations of at least one full period of each teacher every year. When these observations are made, the principal must hold a follow-up conference with the teacher within five days. Strengths, weaknesses and suggestions for improvement must be made and a record of same should be retained in the permanent file of the school and an exact copy given to the teacher."

NAME OF TEACHER OR WORKER _____

COURSE AND GRADE OBSERVED _____ DATE _____

NAME OF APPRAISER _____

Place a check (x) under the column which describes your rating.

	Superior 5 points	Excellent 4 points	Good 3 points	Average 2 points	Fair 1 point	Poor 0 points	Not Observed
I. Appearance and arrangement of classroom							
a. Lighting and ventilation							
b. Plan and flexibility of seating							
c. Utilization of bulletin board(s)							
d. Format and quality of materials displayed							
e. Special features of interest							
f. Other(s) write in:							
Total Points							

II. Teacher

	Superior 5 points	Excellent 4 points	Good 3 points	Average 2 points	Fair 1 point	Poor 0 points	Not Observed
a. General Attitude and personableness of manners							
b. Quality of voice							
c. English usage							
d. Quality of pronunciation							
e. Mastery of materials under consideration							
f. Poise and general consideration							
g. General appearance and appropriateness in dress							
h. Punctual in getting class down to work							
i. Other(s) write in:							
Total Points							

Page 2

III. Procedures and Techniques Used

	Superior 5 points	Excellent 4 points	Good 3 points	Average 2 points	Fair 1 point	Poor 0 points	Not Observed
a. General quality and appropriateness of procedures							
b. Evidence of student-teacher planning							
c. Attention to individual differences							
d. Use of techniques which encourage thinking							
e. Operation of democratic procedure in class							
f. Use of opportunities to make ideas meaningful in the lives of students							
g. Clarity in assignments							
h. Other(s) write in:							
Total Points							

IV. Content, Quality and Significance of Activity

    a. Evidence of readiness for activity

    b. Appropriateness for the grade and abilities of the learners

    c. Accuracy of information

    d. Significance of topics considered

    e. Quality of students' responses

    f. Quality of correlation and integration with other subjects

    g. Opportunities for creative thinking

    h. Other(s) write in:

                      Total Points

V. Others

    a. Wise use of textbooks

    b. Wise use of supplementary materials

    c. Use of chalkboard

    d. Use of bulletin board

    e. Use of library

    f. Use of material center

    g. Use of audio-visual materials

    h. Use of community resources

    i. Other(s) write in:

                      Total Points

VI. General Classroom Climate	Superior 5 points	Excellent 4 points	Good 3 points	Average 2 points	Fair 1 point	Poor 0 points	Not Observed
a. Level of interest							
b. Class participation							
c. Evidence of classroom organization for special responsibilities							
d. Evidence of developing independence and maturity of pupils							
e. Other(s) write in:							
Total Points							

GRAND TOTAL POINTS _____

General comments:

Recommendations to this particular teacher or worker:

114

Byas always spoke up for African American rights.
Correspondence with Congressmen Floyd Hicks and Charles Rangel.

MACON COUNTY BOARD OF EDUCATION
Post Office Box 90
TUSKEGEE, ALABAMA 36083
November 27, 1972

BOARD MEMBERS
DR. P. K. BISWAS, CHAIRMAN
DR. J. H. M. HENDERSON, V. CHAIRMAN
MR. ALLEN ADAMS
DR. ELLIS HALL
MRS. CONSUELLO HARPER

MR. ULYSSES BYAS
SUPERINTENDENT

Representative Floyd B. Hicks
Chairman of the House Armed Services
San Diego Naval Base
San Diego, California

Dear Mr. Hicks:

In reading of the recent disturbances across racial line on the Constellation, the Kitty Hawk and other naval vessels, I feel compelled to register an opinion growing out of some of my personal experiences. I do so with reservations knowing that my experiences in, and subsequent honorable discharge from, the U.S. Navy were activities of some twenty-five or more years ago. I am told that there has been drastic and significant changes since those days of World War II, yet I hear overtones of the same kind of treatment, presumably toward blacks, as many experienced while fighting for democracy during the 1940's.

It was in the winter of 1943 when I was called for induction into the service through the local draft board in Macon, Bibb County, Georgia. In as much as I was enrolled in the senior class I was granted a deferment in order to complete high school.

During the month of July, after receiving my high school diploma, I was inducted into the U.S. Navy at Fort Benning, Georgia and subsequently sent to Jacksonville Naval Air Station for boot training. I was told that I would be either a cook or a cook's helper.

According to my understanding of the then Blue Jacket Manual, the Navy was operating under orders to place all personnel where they were best qualified. It puzzled me for some time that my best qualification placed me in the messmen branch. I learned almost two years later that my official record indicated that I had dropped out of school around the ninth grade. I subsequently had that changed by presenting my high school diploma.

It was aboard the Naval Air Station at Opelika-Dade County, Florida where it was a miracle in a sense, and almost a dehumanizing process that a black could serve his country and at the same time maintain a good record. Four or five examples will suffice.

1. During the 29 months in the navy I was never taught to swim nor how to abandon ship. It is my understanding that on the Naval base there were no facilities for swimming for blacks. The air station did have enlisted men swimming pools.

115

2. For a very long period of time (it seems to me ten, twelve, or fourteen months) all black sailors on station, slept on the top side of an airplane repair hanger. Planes were being repaired around the clock at the hanger which was located at the south end of the runway on the naval base. Furthermore, there were more sailors assigned to those quarters than beds. On many nights several of us wound up sleeping on the floor, this in spite of the fact that there were enlisted men barracks vacant on the base.

3. Motion pictures were shown in the base chapel. It was customary to rope off a section at the extreme back for blacks. Some of us decided that it was too much of a strain on our eyes from that distance and by design, went down towards the front and had seats. After refusing a request from the SP to move, later the Duty Officer came, cocked a pistol at my head, and ordered me to move within five seconds. I am still here.

4. The service which we got at the ship store was through a hole from the screened in front porch. There were tables out there on a porch which faced south and as I recall, was rectangular in shape of about ten to twelve feet wide and twenty feet or more long. Needless to say, whenever unfavorable winds would blow, many times we got wet.

5. When we would enter protest, as we did in the form of a very mild and meek request, we were reminded of the article of war and told that if we persisted we could be charged with mutiny.

In reflecting upon these and other experiences the thought occured to me that the young black sailors serving in the navy today are the sons of my generation. I am sure that some of them are aware of the sufferings of some of us and are, in keeping with the change of time, making their protest somewhat stronger and more pointed than we, yet things, I am told, are different - because of this again I feel constrained to make this sort of backward look.

Then on the other hand when the thought occured to me that those who are now currently in leadership roles, the officers, are also the sons of those who perpetrated evils and other asinine restraints on blacks in the U.S. Navy twenty-five years ago. Could it be that these persons do not like to treat all persons, as are required, equal and to respect the citizenship rights as granted under the Constitution to all of our citizens.

I must say to you, as I said in a hand written letter some years ago to the President of the United States, Franklin Roosevelt, it was most difficult to serve honorably in a navy which attempted to rape the black sailor of his manhood. The sons of my generation know this. I only hope that the

Representative Floyd B. Hicks
Page 3
November 27, 1972

sons of the generation which devised and enforced, under the banner of discipline, the dehumanizing and discriminating rules and regulations upon me and other blacks in the navy twenty-five years ago, are not trying to continue this sort of policy on blacks serving in our U.S. Navy in 1972.

Sincerely,

Ulysses Byas

Ulysses Byas
Superintendent

UB:ps
Copy: Chief of Naval Operation

Congress of the United States

House of Representatives

Washington, D.C. 20515

February 27, 1973

Mr. Ulysses Byas
Superintendent
Macon County Board of
  Education
P.O. Box 90
Tuskegee, Alabama 36083

Dear Mr. Byas:

Although I should have done so earlier, I want
to take this opportunity to thank you for sending me a
copy of the letter you wrote to Congressman Floyd Hicks,
Chairman of the special House Armed Services Committee
investigation into racial problems in the Navy.

I was tremendously impressed, even moved, by
the indelibility of the pain you so eloquently expressed
in your recounting of incidents of racist barbarism
during your own Naval career. Your words were brought
to my mind -- and caused me to reread your letter, by
the aftermath of tragic shooting in New Orleans when
it was revealed that Mark Essex had learned to hate
when in the Navy. You were right in your analysis that the
fault lies not with the young Black men who are protesting
the continuing brutality against them as Black people,
but with a Navy which ignores peaceful protest and responds
only to violence.

The findings of the special investigatory panel,
that the incidents occurred not because of racism, but
because of lax shipboard discipline, were not surprising,
given the nature of the Armed Services Committee. I am
led to wonder, however, whether Floyd Hicks ever read
your letter. If he did, he cannot be easy in conscience
with the findings of his subcommittee.

Sincerely,

Charles B. Rangel
Member of Congress

CBR:p

118

Documents related to the FCC investigation of Alabama
Educational Television and its aftermath.

AFFIDAVIT

COUNTY OF MACON   )
)   SS:
STATE OF ALABAMA   )

        I, Ulysses Byas, being duly deposed, do hereby
state the following:

        1.   That I am Superintendent of Schools for
Macon County, Alabama;

        2.   That I prepared a statement to be submitted
as testimony in the hearing before the F.C.C. concerning
the Alabama Educational Television Commission, Docket Nos.
19422-19430;

        3.   That neither counsel for Petitioners in the
above-referenced matter nor anyone else told me what to
say in this statement;

        4.   That I have read Petitioners' Exhibit No. 29,
and that this is the statement which I prepared.

1/3/73   _Ulysses Byas_
Date   Ulysses Byas

Bernice S. Noble   _Jan 3, 1973_
Notary Public   Date

Affidavit related to Byas's FCC testimony.

119

mailed 1-2-73

mrs Noble

notarize ~~and~~ ~~of~~ attached — make a copy

+ mail original

December 21, 1972

Ulysses Byas
Macon County Board of Education
P. O. Box 90
Tuskegee, Alabama   36083

Dear Mr. Byas:

As I mentioned in my last letter to you, we have
submitted the statement which you prepared as testimony
in the F.C.C. hearing concerning the Alabama
Educational Television Commission. The hearing
has been concluded, and it will not be necessary
for you to make an appearance in Birmingham or
Washington, D. C. to be questioned about the
statement which you made.

However, for the record, it is necessary for us to
supply the F.C.C. with a supporting affidavit. For
your convenience, I have drafted the necessary affidavit and enclosed it with this letter. You will
note that the affidavit makes reference to Petitioners'
Exhibit No. 29, which was the number assigned to your
statement.

I would very much appreciate it if you could have the
enclosed affidavit notarized and returned to me as
soon as possible in the enclosed self-addressed,
stamped envelope.

Again, thanks very much for your time and effort
on this. I believe your statement will be most
helpful to us.

                                    Sincerely,

                                    Lewis J. Paper

PH

Encl

The FCC investigation in process. See pp. 76–79.

1914 SUNDERLAND PL., N.W., WASHINGTON, D.C., 2003b (__2) 296-4238

CITIZENS COMMUNICATIONS CENTER

H RESPONSIVE MEDIA:

January 9, 1975

Mr. Ulysses Byas
Macon County Board of Education
P.O. Box 90
Tuskegee, Alabama

Dear Mr. Byas:

As you may have learned by now, the FCC has
vindicated the right of black citizens to responsive
broadcast service, and has denied license renewal to the
Alabama Educational Television Network. I thought you
might be interested in having a copy of the final
decision, released on January 8, 1975.

Your testimony was invaluable, and, as you
will see, was relied upon by the Commission in determining
that the AETC had failed to serve the needs of Alabama's
black citizens. Everyone involved in the case would like
to thank you for contributing to our ultimate success.

Peace,

Ellen S. Agress

Ellen S. Agress

A. W. STEINEKER, JR.
CHIEF EXAMINER

D. L. BROCK
ASSISTANT CHIEF EXAMINER

STATE OF ALABAMA
DEPARTMENT OF

EXAMINERS OF PUBLIC ACCOUNTS

MONTGOMERY, ALABAMA 36104

TELEPHONE 269-7191

WILLIAM W. DILLARD, JR.
SUPERVISOR COUNTY AUDITS

ROBERT BONNER
SUPERVISOR STATE AUDITS

JAMES W. WEBB
LEGAL COUNSEL

April 24, 1974

Hononable Ulysses Byas
County Board of Education
Macon County
Tuskegee, Alabama

Dear Sir:

Upon completion of an examination of the office of the County Board of Education of Macon County, covering the period from October 1, 1972 through September 30, 1973 the following was found to be due by you:

Increase in salary paid to Superintendent
during a term of office.
Amount paid in this fiscal year---------------$1,249.96

Under the provisions of Act No. 351, General Acts of Alabama 1947, page 231, I, therefore, make formal demand on you for settlement of the above amount.

Very truly yours,

B. M. Burson
Examiner of Public Accounts

Received this the 24th day of April 1974.

Superintendent
Macon County Board
of Education

Demand that a portion of salary be returned to the state. See p. 82.

DEPARTMENT OF EXAMINERS OF PUBLIC ACCOUNTS

MONTGOMERY, ALABAMA 36130

Honorable William W. Dillard, Jr.
Chief Examiner of Public Accounts
Montgomery, Alabama

Dear Sir:

Pursuant to assignment, I have audited the records and accounts of the

County Board of Education
and
Custodian of County School Funds
Macon County, Alabama
October 1, 1973 thru September 30, 1974

Board members for the period under audit are set out on Exhibit #44.

Depository:

At its meeting of November 24, 1970, as recorded on page 72 of the minute book, the Board designated the Alabama Exchange Bank, Tuskegee, Alabama as the depository for all funds of the Macon County Board of E cation.

Audit Scope and Comments:

The minutes of the Board were reviewed with reference to official actions taken during the period under audit. They were neatly prepared, indexed, and appeared to reflect most actions of the Board. Minutes of all meetings were properly approved and signed by the Chairman and Superintendent (as Secretary) of the Board.

The 1973-74 budget was adopted by the Board at its meeting of September 26, 1973, page 71. The budget bore the approval of the State Superintendent of Education under date of December 14, 1973.

All operating fund's bills and accounts were audited for legality and accuracy of extentions and additions. Bills and accounts appeared to have been pre-audited before payment.

Purchases subject to the bid laws (Act 217, Acts of Alabama 1967, page 259, as amended) were verified to bid files maintained in the accounting office.

Revenue from state sources was verified to an abstract taken from state records. Revenue from county and other local sources was verified to official receipts and correspondence on file. All revenues were verified to duplicate deposit slips and traced to applicable journals. Deposits were made timely and intact.

Contracts of teachers and other contracted personnel were examined as to contract amounts, and a determination of amounts due per pay period was made and traced to the October, 1973 payroll. Salaries due each month were verified to the principal's monthly reports, noting the number of days work for which pay was due.

Results from the long audit. See pp. 80-83.

STATE OF ALABAMA—DEPARTMENT OF EXAMINERS OF PUBLIC ACCOUNTS

(Co. Bd. of Ed. and Custodian of Co. Sch. Fds., Macon Co., Ala.)

⌐ck leave taken was verified to sick leave records on file.

After verifying revenues and expenditures of operating funds, all payrolls were added and traced to the various journals. Journals were added and traced to general ledger accounts. Distribution of expenditures was traced to the expenditure ledgers on a test bases to determine that postings had been correctly handled. All accounts were in balance. Cash accounts were reconciled with depository balances as set out on Schedule #1 of Exhibit #1.

Interest bearing warrants and interest coupons becoming due during the year were traced to the warrant register. There were none due and outstanding at the close of the year.

No entries had been posted to the General Fixed Assets Fund during the year under examination. Additions of buildings, improvements other than buildings, furniture and equipment, and school buses and shop equipment were compiled by me from paid invoices and posted to the proper accounts. Deductions resulted from the sale of buses.

There was no detailed audit of Federally funded programs beyond verifying receipts, disbursements and bank reconcilements.

The financial statement for the year was published in the Tuskegee News on October 17, 1974.

Recommendations: None

Charges Against Officials: None

CERTIFICATE:

In my opinion, the accompanying exhibits and related statements of operations, revenues and disbursements present fairly the financial position of the Macon County Board of Education, as of September 30, 1974.

This examination was made in accordance with generally accepted auditing standards and included such tests of the accounting records and such other auditing procedures as were considered necessary in the circumstances.

Respectfully submitted,

Sworn to and subscribed
before me this the 19th
day of November 1975.

Cleo M. Bedsole, Jr.

Henry L. Rogers Jr.
Notary Public

Cleo M. Bedsole, Jr.
Examiner of Public Accounts

EXHIBIT IV

RECOMMENDATIONS

(1) The Minutes indicate that it is presently customary for the Board members to approve the accounts payable in one lump sum. For example, in the Minutes of November 30, 1973, the following is noted: "It was moved by Mrs. Harper and seconded by Mr. Adams that Accounts Payable in the amount of $100,321.73 be approved. The motion passed." The Minutes should reflect not only the total of the accounts payable but should also reflect in detail the names of the individual payees and the amount of money to be paid each payee.

(2) The Minutes of each meeting of the Board of Education should be properly signed by the Secretary of the Board and by the Chairman of the Board after the Board's approval of the Minutes as written by the Secretary. During the period September 4, 1969 through July 30, 1975, the Minutes of the Board meetings on the following dates were not authenticated by either signature: October 5, 1969, December 17, 1969, February 24, 1971, March 24, 1971, November 24, 1972, June 25, 1975, July 23, 1975 and July 30, 1975. One of the two necessary signatures was missing for the meetings of May 18, 1970, May 22, 1970, May 29, 1970, June 15, 1970, July 29, 1970, August 6, 1970 and February 10, 1975. It is recommended that the attention of the Board Secretary and the Board Chairman be given to this responsibility for each Board meeting.

(3) In accordance with Act No. 1775 of the Legislature of the State Government, approved September 17, 1971, the Superintendent of Education must devote his entire time to public school business of Macon County. It is recommended that whenever it is necessary for the Superintendent to conduct official business of the Macon County Board of Education outside of Macon County that specific permission be given by the Board for any such travel. It was not found in the Board Minutes where such

Recommendations from the Auditors, 1976

permission was granted. Permission by the Board for the Superintendent to travel outside Macon County should also include provisions for actual necessary expenses.

(4) A mailing list of bidders should be maintained on the invitations to bid that are mailed on each item that is submitted to bid. Invitations to bid should be mailed early enough to allow all bidders time to compute their bid and return it before the scheduled bid opening. Invitations to bid should be mailed to at least three qualified bidders and more if practical, to insure receiving the lowest possible bid for the service or material desired.

(5) Action should be taken to insure that all materials and services are received before a payment is made. This could be accomplished by having a designated place on the purchase order for the person receiving the materials or services to sign. Preferably a receiving report should be made up by the individual receiving an item. This receiving report should be completed in duplicate, with the copy being retained by the individual receiving the item or service, the original going to the Custodian of Funds to be attached to the voucher for payment, which is then retained in the permanent file.

At the end, some dreams went unfulfilled, but many
people appreciated what Byas had done.

DREAM

GUIDELINES FOR THE DESIGN OF A COMPREHENSIVE HIGH SCHOOL

FOR

MACON COUNTY, ALABAMA

The following statement is the philosophy of education of the

Macon County Board of Education:

> The Macon County Board of Education is dedicated to providing
> the educational opportunities and experiences needed for each
> child under its charge to attain his maximum intellectual and
> social fulfillment.

> In keeping with this dedication, the Board incorporates into
> its operational philosophy these three precepts:

> 1. A child is the most precious resource of our
>   society; as such he is fully entitled to the
>   best education program society can devise.

> 2. Each child is unique in both his readiness for
>   and propensity toward fulfilling his own potential;
>   accordingly, his educational needs may be unique
>   at any given point in time and must be accommodated
>   as such.

> 3. The role of the school in the total development
>   of the child is so significant that the Board
>   feels ethically obligated to accept as satisfactory
>   nothing less than professional excellence in either
>   its own actions or in the actions of any of its
>   employees.

> In manifesting this philosophy, the Board shall constantly
> examine and announce operational and programatic objectives
> and priorities for the Public Schools of Macon County.

> In keeping with the above philosophy, it is believed that the

following must be incorporated into the planning and design of a com-

prehensive high school to serve the needs of the children of Macon County.

Byas's thoughts about a new high school. See p. 101.

127

- The total physical plant for this comprehensive high school
  will accomodate 2,000 students - grades nine - up.

- The concept of the open school will be incorporated into the
  operational structure of the school, including not only the
  regular scheduling of classes, but with the idea that the
  school will be open from 6 a.m. to 10 p.m. with students
  allowed to register for a maximum of 6 courses throughout the
  day - all courses will be offered throughout the total day
  for anyone to take part, thereby establishing a Continuing
  Education Program in conjunction with the required courses
  of academic study.

- The physical plant must be planned and designed not only to
  meet utiliterian needs but should encompass the esthetic as
  well as comfort with each area being decorated and furnished
  as to be suggestive of the kind of subject matter to be dealt
  with in each given area.

- Wherever possible, throughcut school building, there should
  be rooms equipped with one-way glass so in-service training
  personnel can observe demonstrative and masterful teaching.

- The physical pant should be so constructed as to handle two
  main entrances at different levels - Bus area for loading and
  unloading should be at a different area.

- There should be a sub-basement area to house emergency shelter
  quarters with emergency storage of food for 1,000 persons for
  48 hours.

- Faculty/Workers Parking Area to accomodate 150 cars.

- Visitors parking area to accomodate 150 cars.

- The campus surrounding the physical plant should include:

     . . General purpose track, field and football stadium
          to seat 10,000.
     . . Outdoor pool
     . . Baseball and Softball fields
     . . Tennis courts, volley Ball courts, Shuffleboard courts,
          Badminton Courts, and others as appropriate. (These can
          be constructed on asphalt surface which can also serve
          as a general purpose parking lot.

. . Botanical Garden

. . Small animal zoo

. . Small lake

The following represents the guidelines for the design of the actual physical plant of the comprehensive high school.

SCIENCE AREA

   2 General Biology Labs - 30 Students each
   Environmental Studies Lab - 25 Students
   2 Chemistry Labs - 25 Students each
   1 Physics Lab - 25 Students
   Marine Biology Lab - 25 Students
   Meteorology Lab - 25 Students
   Anatomy/Physiology Lab - 25 Students

COMMUNICATIONS AREA

   Journalism Lab Room (off-set press, etc.) - 20 Students
   T.V. Production Room - 15 Students - with closed circuit T.V.
      in all classrooms
   Photography.Classroom/Lab - 15 Students
   Computer Room for teaching computer techniques with terminals
      throughout classrooms and/or laboratories and required.

COMMERCIAL/BUSINESS AREA

   1 Beginning Typing room - 75 Students each
   1 Advanced Typing room - 30 Student
   General Office Practice Room with adjoining room for repro-
      duction equipment (Ditto, Xerox, Mimeograph, etc.)
   Accounting - 20 Students
   Bookkeeping - 20 Students
   Merchandising/Selling - 15 Students
   Consumer Buying - 15 Students
   Real Estate

SOCIAL SCIENCE

   Sociology
   Psychology

History
Anthropology/Lab - Classroom
Room capable of being converted into mock courtroom

HOME ECONOMICS AREA

2 Suites each with capacity for 20 containing complete:
    Kitchen
    Living Room
    Dining Room
1 Sewing Room - 20 Students
Interior Decoration - 20 Students

MATHEMATICS LAB

60 Students

LANGUAGE LAB

75 Students

MUSIC DEPARTMENT

Orchestra Room   *Voice*
Band Room   *Piano*
Choir - 75 Students
Instrument Repair Lab - 10-12 Students
Individual Practice Rooms - 20 Students

PHYSICAL EDUCATION AREA

Spectator Sport Gymnasium to seat 4,000
All purpose gymnasium for teaching only 100 students
Swimming Pool
Locker Rooms

FIRST AID CLINIC

DEPARTMENT FOR BUILDING MAINTAINANCE CREW

Including lockers/showers

CAREER EDUCATION

     Upholstery - 15 Students
     Brick Masonry - 15 Students
     Auto Mechanics - 15 Students
     Radio/TV Repair - 15 Students
     Pre-Flight Training - 15 Students
     Airplane Mechanics - 15 Students
     Mechanical Drawing - 15 Students
     Airplane Linesmen - 15 Students
     Tailoring/Dressmaking - 15 Students
     Cabinet Making

House wiring
Plumbing
House construction

PARA-MEDICAL AREA

     Para-Medic Training - 10-15 Students
     Pre-Vet Training - 12 Students
     Pre-Nursing - 10-15 Students
     Pre-Dentistry - 10-15 Students
     Laboratory Technicians - 10-15 Students

FINE ARTS AREA

     Painting
     Drawing
     Ceramics/Kiln
     Sculpture
     Pre-Architecture
     Drafting
     Little Theatre (1,000 capacity)
        Prop room
        Make-up/Dressing Rooms
        Wardrobe area

CONTINUING EDUCATION AREA

     Bookbinding
     Leathercraft
     Woodworking

LIBRARY

    2 Major Sections
     a. media: listening to tapes and observing audio/visua
        material
     b. Books/Reference/Research/Periodicals

AUDITORIUM

    4,000 Seating Capacity

CAFETERIA (Restaruant Type)

    Central Kitchen with provision for variety food preparation
    Four (4) serving lines

OFFICE SUITES

    Administration
    Counselors
    Social Workers

FACULTY/STUDENT LOUNGES

TEACHER WORKROOMS (FOR CLASS PREPARATION)

ACCOUNT RECEIVING/INVENTORY/DISTRIBUTION CENTER

GENERAL PURPOSE CLASSROOMS, AS NEEDED

EARLY CHILDHOOD DEVELOPMENT LABORATORY

    This area will accomodate approximately 75 babies: ages
    2 wks. - 4 yrs.
    2 wks. - 6 mos. - 25 infants
    6 mos. - 2 yrs. - 25 babies
    2 yrs. - 4 yrs. - 25 toddlers.

R. O. T. C. AREA *- Security Storage Room*

    400 Students

MACON COUNTY BOARD OF EDUCATION
Post Office Box 90
TUSKEGEE, ALABAMA 36083

December 19, 1976

A Tribute to Dr. Ulysses Byas

"An Eagle's Eye View or a
Bug's Eye View"

Many of us are too close to the ground like the bug and see
only sticks, rocks and dirt. You are fortunate, for you are
able to soar like the eagle, see the big picture and also have
the visual acuity to see where the small pieces fit into the
arrangement. Dr. Byas, your perception of the world of work
is phenomenal and may be likened to that of Dr. George Washington
Carver, Dr. Booker T. Washington and Dr. Leon Sullivan in many
ways.

When you answered our call in 1970, it was much like the time
in 1896 when George Washington Carver answered the call to
come to Tuskegee Institute. Booker T. Washington had called
him and told him of the challenges and opportunities of working
here at Tuskegee. He discussed the lack of resources in terms
of physical plant and funds, but built the case on the need for
help in the education of youth. He stressed the training of
the hands as well as the head to do the common things in an
uncommon way.

When we called you in the spring of 1970, it was after searching
the country from California to Georgia, for the best man that we
could find for the job. Our call paralleled that of Dr. Booker
T. Washington to Dr. George Washington Carver. We discussed the
paucity of resources, the state of our physical plant, our
indebtedness to the extent that we were almost insolvent and the
fact that we could pay a superintendent only $12,000 by law.
You took a reduction in pay to come to a most difficult job.

Your long time dream of helping build an area Vocational Education
Center for Macon County, did not materialize, although it was
considered by you and the previous board to be the biggest local
step forward that public education could make at this time.
Nevertheless, you continue to operate in the realm with the
eagle's eye view. You are a success as defined by Dr. Booker
T. Washington. "Success is to be measured not so much by the
position that one has reached in life as by the obstacles which
he has overcome while trying to succeed."

When you came to our school system, we had short-term indebtedness in excess of one-half of our total annual local income and had a very questionable credit rating. The Board was unable to meet several payrolls during the 1969-70 school year while state auditors raised many questions and even made some charges against officials, questioning purchases and the prudent use of funds. The Accounting Department consisted of several ladies, typewriters, paper, pencils and desk-top calculators. Moreover, the authorization for collecting local taxes was to expire in seven years which precluded borrowing money through bonds and warrants. You as Superintendent and the Board were determined, even in those adverse conditions, that significant improvements in the quantity and quality of the system could be made. An austerity program with tight financial controls to assure the best possible use of limited available resources was implemented. As a result of that Policy, several significant improvements have been made throughout the school system. Inclusive among the improvements are the following:

I. Physical Plant Improvements:

Complete renovation of one main building at Institute High School, Washington Public, Tuskegee Public and Lewis Adams - new roofs over entire building at Shorter Gym, South Macon High, Tuskegee Public, Lewis Adams, East Macon, Notasulga Gym and auditorium and two buildings at Institute High School. Interior and exterior painting and plumbing improvements. At a cost of $575,000.00 an addition of 13 classrooms, a kitchen and cafeteria were added to the D. C. Wolfe plant; and a $650,000.00 addition is 70% completed at the South Macon plant. The Wolfe construction was paid for from local funds upon completion.

II. Finance and Inventory Accounting:

A computerized system of finance and inventory accounting was purchased and installed. We have the capability of determining at anytime in the budget year, just how we are progressing with income, expenses and inventory level of all properties owned by the Board of Education.

III. Personnel:

The following new positions were created and staffed:

a. Central Office: Assistant Superintendent of Education; Director of Curriculum and Instruction; Director of Personnel, Research and Property; Coordinator of Special Education; Coordinator of In-Service and Textbook Coordinator.

      b. Local Schools: Guidance Counselors in High Schools; Librarians in all schools; Secretaries for all schools; additional custodial help; assistant coaches for female students and full-time assistant principals at three schools.

  IV. Instructional Support:

All student fees were eliminated and selling and solicitation involving students were prohibited. Local schools are allotted funds in excess of the State's minimum for the purchase of instructional supplies. The allocation for the purchase of library materials exceeds the requirement of the Regional Accrediting Association and special allotments are made to local schools for travel, ROTC and the instrumental music program.

  V. Professional Improvement through In-Service:

A model In-Service Improvement Program through mini-courses was designed and implemented. In addition, an initial Leadership Development Workshop was initiated.

  VI. School Board Policies:

In 1971, for the first time the Board of Education developed written policies. That manual was completely revised during the 1974-75 school year.

  VII. School Consolidation:

Tuskegee High School consoldated into Institute High School; Chambliss Children's House closed; Prairie Farms building abandoned; and the Shorter School was eliminated as a separate administrative unit.

  VIII. Special Programs:

Proposals were developed and implemented in several areas. Drop-out Prevention, approximately 1.3 million dollars over a four year period; Preparation for Parenthood, $560,000.00 over a five year period; ESAA approximately $600,000.00 over a five year period. Other continuing programs which were refunded includes, Follow Through approximately three million dollars over six years, Title I approximately three million dollars over six years, Head Start, 2.5 million dollars over six years. Several smaller grants for other purposes were obtained and programs implemented.

  IX. Curriculum:

Instrumental Music Program was started at three High Schools (Wolfe, Notasulga, South Macon) and additional instruments purchased for Tuskegee Institute High School. Each local

faculty is studying and outlining courses, at all grade
levels, in connection with our self-evaluation. The
construction of an Area Vocational School has been
approved by all legal agencies as required by law and
$200,000.00 of flow-through the State Federal funds
have been granted to help with the construction cost.
The Architectural plans through schematic drawings have
been completed.

The above are suggestive of the improvements which have been made
in the Macon County School System during the last six and one-half
years. All schools now meet or exceed the minimum quantitative
standard of the Regional Accrediting Committee. Only the completion
of the self-study physical plant improvements that are already
budgeted and a review by a Visiting Committee stand in the way of
full accreditation of all Schools in Macon County. Moreover, the
renewal of county-wide school taxes makes it possible for the
Board to secure funds through Bonds and Warrants for capitol
improvements. We have within our reach the resources to build
an area vocational education center and make necessary repairs
on all physical plants.

Throughout this period the Board has met all payrolls and bills
payable without borrowing any funds and has paid off all previous
indebtedness. Although some of the funds are obligated, this
past fiscal year ended (9-30-76) with a balance of $675,000.00.

Although we have been audited repeatedly and in one case under
constant audit for nine months, all audits have shown outstanding
fiscal management.

Dr. Byas it has been a real source of pleasure working with you.
We in Macon County have been richly blessed by your leadership.

Ellis Hall

P.K. Biswas

Consuella J. Harper

Allen M. Adams

Joe M. Hender

136

Index